C000067785

City Slackers

Workers of the World ...
You Are Wasting Your Time!

Steve McKevitt

CYANBOOKS

Copyright © 2006 Swell Ideas Ltd

First published in 2006 by Cyan Books, an imprint of:

Cyan Communications Limited
119 Wardour Street
London W1F 0UW
United Kingdom
T: +44 (0)20 7565 6120
E: sales@cyanbooks.com
www.cyanbooks.com

A CIP record for this book is available from the British Library

ISBN-13 978-1-904879-72-5
ISBN-10 1-904879-72-1

Designed and typeset by Cambridge Publishing Management Limited

Printed and bound in Great Britain by
Creative Print & Design Group (Wales), Ebbw Vale

For Niamh, Evan and Aoife

Acknowledgements

I would like to acknowledge gratefully the assistance of the following people who helped me while I was putting this book together: Brendan for his editorial insight, Stuart for his input in Chapter 2, and finally Ciaran and Fiona for patiently reading through the various drafts.

I'd also like to thank everybody else who provided me with City Slacker anecdotes, but who asked me to respect their right to anonymity (you know who you are).

Contents

Foreword

Life's not fair! Surely this must be one of the most important and unpleasant lessons of childhood (well, mine, anyway). Our parents may sit us down after a tearful and unwarranted trauma – the loss of a pet or misplacement of a favourite toy – and shatter our faith in the concept of natural justice by explaining that things don't always go our way. They call it part of growing up. We learn that the good guys don't always win, that we don't always get our ball back, that we can't have our cake and eat it, that bullies don't always get their comeuppance, and that the bad guys sometimes get away with it too, regardless of the machinations of a few meddling kids. This is a very pessimistic view of the world perhaps, but one that is intended to stand us in good stead as we deal with life's inevitable disappointments and its habit of pissing on bonfires, raining on parades and bursting party balloons.

There is, of course, another way of looking at this fact of life. Rather than dwelling on it as a bad thing, or simply viewing it pragmatically, there are many who will see it as an opportunity to be grasped enthusiastically. If some people are going to get less than their fair share of luck, shouldn't we be looking to be one of those individuals who get more? After all, the world is full of people doing much better than they deserve and consumers of the mass media don't have to look very hard for supporting evidence. In newspapers and magazines and on TV we see famous people – who are not really famous for very much at all – living fabulous lives. Whether it's singing songs, looking nice in a frock, taking their top off, dancing in time to music, reading an autocue, or almost having sex with someone they've known for five minutes on a reality TV show, people, it would seem, want to be famous. They just don't know what they want to be famous for.

That so many people seem to be getting on in life without actually being good at anything at all might be an inevitable part of western society, but the fact is, this is not a malaise exclusive to the famous. The world of celebrity provides a highly visible cadre of slackers for whom the working day seems to revolve around nothing more than which car to drive, where to shop, who to have lunch with or what party to go to. But away from the glare of the media, in the corporate world there is an even greater number who have realized that presentation really is more important than substance. These people are building hugely successful careers based on this premise. For them, their employer is no more than a vehicle to further their personal ambition. If the company's objectives fit in with their own, then all well and good, but more often than not they don't. These individuals may hold senior positions already, but certainly they will be on the lookout for impressive high-powered jobs. Some of them are even running big companies. These are the City Slackers: the people who know that it ain't what you do, it's the way that you do it. *You* could be one of them. Or, if you prefer, you *could* be one of them.

Since I started work, I've found examples of company or individual incompetence as interesting as I have found those about corporate brilliance. There is a view that you can learn more from failure than you can from success.

One of the first jobs I had after leaving university was as a temp in what was then called the Department of Employment head office. I spent most of my time at the photocopier making coffee or typing up presentations in WordPerfect 3.0 on the office pre-Windows PC. The office was open plan and seating was fiercely non-hierarchical (even if nothing else was), which explains how I found myself sitting opposite my line manager's line manager, Tony Mariner. Tony was a higher executive officer (HEO). Away from head office this position carried a lot of responsibility. In the field, HEOs would be running unemployment benefit offices and Jobcentres with dozens of staff reporting to them. Here at head office, however, Tony was responsible for … well, I was only there for six months so I never found out, but I think it might have had something to do with binding.

There were many things to admire about the way that Tony conducted himself, not least the shameless way that he took a post-prandial, 20-minute nap at his desk every afternoon. Tony spent the remainder of his day writing down interesting facts in his "big book of facts" (I'm not joking). He was a keen pub quiz player and, he explained to me, every time he heard a fact he'd never come across before, he wrote it down in his big book so that it could be recalled whenever needed. The only break in this rigorous schedule came on a Friday, when he arranged his weekend's rambling activity in the Yorkshire dales. What Tony never seemed to spend time doing was any work. Organizing an attempt on the Pennine Way, yes – work, no.

Interesting though Tony's story is, he and people like him are not the subject of this book. Tony was just a lazy sod. Everybody could see that "Ridgewalker Tony" was a skiver, so no one took him seriously. Had he behaved like that in the private sector he probably would have been fired, but he got away with it, largely because nobody could be bothered to do anything about it. Tony Mariner is not a new social phenomenon. He is not a City Slacker.

The City Slacker is a different animal altogether. Born in the late 1980s Thatcherite boom, the City Slacker has evolved into a complex beast: loyalty-free, utterly self-serving and in fact about as effective as Tony on an off-day. But the perception of the City Slacker among peers and seniors will be very different indeed. The ultimate company man, first in and last out, you can depend on him to burn the midnight oil putting the finishing touches to an important strategy document or vital presentation. It's not unusual to get emails and telephone calls from him late at night or over the course of the weekend. Often he'll be the first to volunteer for projects outside his remit or at least be ready to offer insight, support and good advice.

The inspiration for *City Slackers* came from two sources. In summer 2003 I was invited to produce a series of columns about marketing in the entertainment industry. One of these involved looking specifically at the role of product and brand managers. As I was writing the article I was struck by two things: first, just how many brand and product managers there are; second, how difficult it was in many cases to identify exactly what they were responsible for, in the tangible, adding value sense.

The following spring I had a number of conversations about this subject with a friend of mine who works in marketing. We coined the phrase "City Slacker" to describe an individual in an organization who wields authority but has no accountability. Partly for our own amusement we sketched out a profile of the ultimate City Slacker: an individual with a track record for nothing but failure, who enjoys a high-rolling career nonetheless. Once we'd applied our model to the real world, it became very easy to find parallels and the idea for the book was born.

The examples and anecdotes included in *City Slackers* are all true. They are either from my own experience or were first-hand accounts told to me by one of the many people I interviewed. In all cases, I have changed the names of the individuals or companies involved. While this might make *City Slackers* a slightly less salacious read than it might have been, I hope it is no less entertaining for this. Some of these stories are shocking, but a lot of them are very funny and I hope I have done the original tellers justice with my written interpretations. Another reason for the use of pseudonyms is that I have no desire to conduct a witch-hunt or hurt anybody's feelings, and I believe that the evidence for a phenomenon that is much more widespread than the examples I have included here is undeniable and you won't have to look very hard to find enough of them to fill this book 100 times over.

Steve McKevitt
SoYo, March 2006

1 | **City Slickers**

In June 1983 I left school, albeit briefly, at the age of 16. Up to this point, I'd had an unremarkable academic career and the popular view, that I was a bright but lazy student, was supported by a steady stream of "Could do better" school reports. At least I was consistent.

In an attempt to prove them all wrong, and in anticipation of a miserable set of O-level results, my dad pulled a few strings at his place of work and managed to secure me an apprenticeship as a tiler. Not, I hasten to add, the kitchen-and-bathroom variety of tiler but the industrial shopping-centre-and-swimming-pool variant. Thus was I reassured that, should my academic performance live down to expectations, at least I would be guaranteed gainful employment and the exciting prospect of learning a trade that was considered both manly and honest.

Would that my conduct, during what turned out to be a mere 12 weeks of unrelenting misery and back-breaking hard work, could be described as manly and honest. My simpering performance was feeble.

We were reflooring a milk factory – all 90,000 square feet of it. The first shock was that the factory owner was not prepared to stop production while we replaced the floor. This meant that the working day started at 2.00 in the afternoon and finished at 10.30 at night – just after closing time.

The "we" was me and two Liverpudlian tilers in their mid-50s, Sid and Christy. These two wits were delighted to have the boss's son labouring on their behalf and after a week's induction, which consisted largely of the inevitable errands for glass hammers and left-handed screwdrivers, we got down to work properly. Sid's nickname was "Catweazel", and I quickly found out that this was as much to do with his fear of "electrickery" as it was his dishevelled appearance. The first half of his and Christy's day consisted of sitting on milk crates, reading the *Sun* and exchanging gags about my suspect sexuality (I'd foolishly admitted to liking the music of The Smiths) while I crawled under the machinery, protected by just a New Order T-shirt and shorts, set about chopping up the floor with a jackhammer and loaded all the rubble into a wheelbarrow. The machinery was less than five feet off the ground, which made standing up impossible. Every activity had to be conducted in a kneeling or crouching position. After 20 minutes the build-up of lactic acid made my thighs and upper arms ache unbearably, but at least it blotted out the pain in my knees and back. To give yourself an idea of what it was like, next time you're digging the garden, try doing it in a kneeling position for four or five hours.

Breaking up the floor released a sea of rancid milk that had collected over 30 years and a stench that was overpowering; to this day, the smell of milk is enough to make me want to retch. It was also a smell that lingered and, as a result, rapidly became a dominant feature of my wardrobe. Needless to say, meeting girls became difficult. Of course, it wasn't all ripping up floors; there was cement to be mixed, tiles to be carried and endless trips with wheelbarrows full of rubble to the skip a mere quarter of a mile away.

Whether it was part of my father's master plan to get me back into education or not, it succeeded. Within a month I'd decided that whatever happened, I was going back to school in the autumn. Sitting behind a desk and offering creative excuses for failing to complete assignments took on an air of new-found glamour. Finding out that I'd scraped through seven O-levels – against all odds – was one of the biggest celebration days of my life, I was even singing while I filled the wheelbarrow that afternoon. And so it was that I turned my back on the world of manly and honest toil to rejoin my old schoolmates at sixth form. For the first time in my life, I began studying hard.

Five years later, with the milk factory now an incoherent memory, I was armed with a 2:2 in politics and back in the job market. I had given very little thought to what I was going to do to earn a living, beyond the fact that it should be indoor work with no heavy lifting. In search of inspiration, I paid several visits to my university's amiable careers adviser, Miss McInnerney, and gave her the brief that I was willing to do "anything but construction". Over the course of a month or so, we spent a series of half-hour sessions trying to identify an appropriate career. After the initial diagnostic session was out of the way, which identified my strengths (indoor work) and weaknesses (physical), we developed a system. Chloë (we'd got to know each other quite well by then) would run through a list of possibilities, I would ask for more details, she would do her best to give me a job overview and I would dismiss them as unappealing. At last Chloë, who was clearly running out of patience with my stock "What's that?

Hmmm … not really" response, finally pulled the rabbit out of the hat: "Have you ever thought about marketing, Steve?" The honest answer was: I hadn't. Not ever. Not only had I not thought of it, I didn't know anyone else who had. None of my friends at school or college had ever talked about working in marketing or the media, or advertising or PR. My dad's career advice consisted of suggesting periodically that I take "a fresh look at accountancy" and my school careers teacher, Mr Breen, certainly hadn't talked about it – although to be fair, unless it was to do with woodwork, the Midland Bank or the Royal Engineering Corps, he didn't really talk about anything. Even the computer program, which promised to determine your ideal job, that was a fixture of my sixth form college's careers library, hadn't mentioned it. (This was my first experience, in what is an ever-lengthening line, of technology failing to live up to expectations; the program determined my ideal job as "forester".)

One kid at school wanted to be a journalist. We assumed he was shooting for a gig with our local weekly paper, the *Ormskirk Advertiser*, but even a career covering girl guides handing over cheques, weddings and school football seemed, well, a bit beyond the likes of us, so we dismissed him as a fantasist. Back then, getting a job in the media seemed about as achievable as becoming an astronaut.

As it transpired, Chloë knew very little about it either, but one thing was clear: it was indoor work with no heavy lifting and it sounded like it might be interesting. I like to think that I didn't choose marketing, it chose me.

Now, if my career choice sounds a little phlegmatic, you need to realize what growing up in small-town northern England in the 1980s was like. The 1980s was a pretty miserable decade. It began with the realization that the post-war boom, built on the "mixed economy" theories of Keynes and delivered by a succession of consensus governments responsible for fuelling the misplaced optimism of the 1960s, had finally crashed and burned.

Social experiments in housing, education and public welfare, the pitiful performance of nationalized industries, experimental town planning, festering industrial relations and ham-fisted economic management by bureaucrats had all contributed in their own way. The economy looked shot, with mass unemployment its key feature; inner city riots were commonplace and international relations took place against a perceived backdrop of nuclear holocaust. In short, growing up in the 1980s you were convinced that you were never going to get a job, but it didn't matter because we'd all be dead anyway. And at least The Smiths had a new album coming out.

How different things were looking seven years later. Thatcher's bloody paradigm shift to an unfettered free market had been achieved and with it had come a similarly stark change in social values. This new economy seemed to depend largely on exporting money, and a new breed of worker had evolved to work within it: this was the age of the City Slicker. With hindsight, the upturn itself was a period of transition: a hiatus between the death of the old economy based on heavy industry and its replacement, a service economy that would achieve stability and growth through rapid advances in information technology and digital communications.

These were much simpler times. City Slickers may have had red braces, a filofax and ponytail, their Shibboleth may have been just making money, and they may have claimed to believe that "greed is good" and "lunch is for wimps", but underneath they were still old-fashioned people. They referred to Channel 4 as the "new channel", thought that the fax machine was a pretty neat invention and almost certainly employed someone to do their typing for them (although probably on a modern electric typewriter) while they read their copy of *Today*: an amazing newspaper with coloured blobs rather than black-and-white pictures. The internet, if they knew about it at all, was a place where science students played text versions of Dungeons and Dragons, surfing was an activity people did at the beach, and football was run by people who knew that you could never turn clubs into real businesses, still played on a Saturday and watched exclusively by the hoi polloi.

The commercial world has changed beyond recognition in the last 20 years. Business success has never been more difficult to sustain than it is today. The rapid evolution in technology provides companies with an overwhelming number of strategic opportunities in the new economies. Backing the wrong horse can be disastrous; household names such as WHSmith and Marks & Spencer are seeing their share prices mauled and profits eroded. And it's not just the big corporates that are feeling the pinch. Many of the bright young ventures started by bright young things at the turn of the century are trading at a fraction of their high-tide valuation. That is, of course, if they're still trading at all.

The real problem, some say, is that "managers no longer know how to manage."*

But it's not all gloom. The rewards for failure have never been greater than they are in the twenty-first century service economy. Six-figure packages for the mediocre performance of senior executives have become something of a norm. So much so that, in September 2004, the £3.8 million† pay-off awarded to departing Sainsbury's CEO Peter Davies – who, incidentally, had singularly failed to make an iota of difference to the company's performance – brought this comment from the *Observer's* Business Editor Frank Kane:

> I cannot go along with the way the latest Sainsbury's fiasco has been interpreted. Sir Peter Davies settled for less than his contractual rights, knocking around £1 million off his shares entitlement and mitigating his salary claims. He ends up with £3 million, less than he could have asked his lawyers to push for. Rather magnanimous of him, actually, and a recognition of the effort he has put into

---

*Source: the *Guardian*, 22.10.05 ("Is the hired help just a rip-off?", Matt Keating) Given that the "some" in this case are management consultants, who make a living by claiming to be able to teach managers how to manage, you may think this smacks of coming up with a cure and then identifying a disease.

†Source: the *Observer*, 03.10.04 ("Sainsbury's £10m monopoly game", Sarah Ryle). The pay-off was variously reported between £3 million and £3.8 million.

Sainsbury's. The task of turning round the ailing supermarket business was beyond his ability, but maybe it would have defeated anyone.*

It's interesting to think that if the task "would have defeated anyone", then arguably you or I could have been equally as successful in this role and, no doubt, would be crying all the way to the bank. (Had it been me failing at Sainsbury's instead of Davies then rest assured you would now be staring at an empty page.)

The culture of failure runs from top to bottom in most large modern businesses. With so little room for success, the smart people are those who make rapid progress in their careers by being seen as a safe pair of hands. Despite the fact that nobody is actually making anything anymore, there's still plenty of work to be done.

The best way to avoid failure is to stop trying to succeed, and most companies of a reasonable size have enough soft projects for you to cut your teeth on without ever having to worry about producing something, achieving anything or – God forbid – actually making a difference. There's more than enough corporate rebranding, strategic realignment, market analysis, brand development, product messaging and public relations to keep you busy before you need to take up a role with real accountability. And by that time you'll have a lucrative failure reward or exit package to look forward to.

---

*Source: the *Observer*, 19.09.04 ("The inspectors should call at Jarvis", Frank Kane).

But in the meantime, kick back and relax: the age of the City Slicker is dead. We are now living in the age of the City Slacker.

It's nearly 20 years since I left university and started my career. By some standards, I suppose, I've been reasonably successful. My generation has a unique perspective: we are old enough to remember what offices were like before computers arrived, but we were young enough to be able to embrace the changes in the working environment without being intimidated. What we should find staggering is the expansion in service sector jobs. Marketing, PR and sales departments are now huge and this has led in turn to a massive increase in the huge growth of the number of companies to service them: advertising agencies, design agencies, PR consultancies, market research specialists, media trainers, brand developers, creative consultants, web labs, communications suppliers, copywriters, freelancers, media buyers, new media specialists, producers, management consultants, business planners and marketing strategists.

In 1993 I joined a medium-sized video games publisher as PR manager. There were four people in the marketing department. We employed a small local creative agency and the biggest component of my budget was postage and photographic reproduction. By the time I left in 1999, we were still a medium-sized video games publisher, but the marketing department had grown to over 20 people, with two heavyweight London ad agencies and three retained PR agencies. True, the market had changed, we were now spending millions of pounds in marketing and we would certainly have needed a few more people, but with hindsight we weren't five times better or three times as effective. There were a lot more internal meetings though. To offset this massive operational cost I had, thankfully, clawed back a couple of thousand quid a year by storing images digitally and distributing them by email.

Back in the 1980s it was not unusual to take a relaxed approach to what you were going to do after graduation. Less than 15% of the population were given the opportunity to study – they even paid you to do it. Not unusually, I was the first person in my entire family to secure a place at university and was paraded around proud grandparents, aunts and uncles (all of whom, on hearing I was to study politics, quipped: "Are you going to be prime minister then?") by my even prouder parents, like a returning war hero.

As I said, they were simpler times.

Going to university today is fast becoming the mode rather than the average. By 2008, it is estimated that the number of school-leavers entering higher education will reach 56%, exceeding the government's 50% target. They will leave three years later with an average debt of £12,400 and, in most cases, unrealistic expectations. Today's generation of graduates expect to have interesting and glamorous lives and a big part of that is having an interesting or glamorous job. PR is now the most popular target profession for undergraduates, many of whom see it as an endless round of launch parties, drinking free bottled beer on parquet floors while arranging a cover story with Richard or Rebekah. You might be interested to know that there are more media studies students than there are jobs in the media. I don't believe there's anybody who thinks that the increase in student numbers has led to an increase in standards, but despite the previous comment, the employment rate among media studies graduates is very high in comparison to other subjects. Why?

The simple fact is that there are many more jobs in the media/marketing sector than ever before. WHSmith stocks over 4,500 different publications each month: there are now hundreds of TV and digital radio channels and hundreds of thousands of commercial websites, all of whom rely on advertising for revenue and PR for content. All of this provides more and more opportunities for companies to push products, messages and services. For very small companies who have never previously considered pushing a message, a few thousand pounds spent on a modest PR campaign can produce results. In the UK last year over £2.5 billion was spent on PR alone. That's a lot of people ringing a lot of people.

There are many indicators for the growth of the service sector during the last 20 years. I decided to conduct my own research using that essential stalker's handbook and old flame-rekindling hearth, Friends Reunited (www.friendsreunited.com). Logging on to my old school records, I was pleased to see that well over half of my old school year had decided to leave an upbeat, chirpy message about themselves. Scanning through the professions of a group of people brought few surprises. Those one had expected to be high-flying indeed were; those one had expected to perform less impressively either had not heard about the site or had decided against posting. And my old friend Andy, who sat next to me in French and allowed me to copy his work during our mock O-level, had turned out to be gay after all.

The Class of '82 were earning a living as engineers, accountants, lawyers, teachers, police officers, IT specialists, entrepreneurs, construction workers, civil servants and retail managers. Not one of them was working in the media, marketing or PR and only a small percentage had put themselves through higher education. This was in stark contrast to the Class of '99. Almost everybody who posted had attended a course at university and while many were working as teachers or engineers, many more had found employment as account executives, product marketers, PRs, journalists, production assistants, web designers, graphic artists, buyers or even management consultants.

This may not be a particularly scientific experiment, but it sits well with my own experience. As I write I'm still on the right side of 40, and earn a living in what is generously described as the media and communications sector. My work brings me into contact with all kinds of organizations: publishers, broadcasters, designers, advertising and PR agencies, mobile communications companies, DVD and video games publishers and the like. It is rare that I encounter anyone much older than myself, but not unusual to meet someone ten years younger in a role that carries an enormous amount of responsibility. I have been involved with several large organizations that are run by boards of directors all very much younger than myself.

At this point you might be tempted to think, "So what?" There are more jobs in marketing and the media than ever before, there are more people who want to do these jobs and there are more people "training" to do them than ever before. Perfect. Except ... except, well, don't tell anyone this, but none of it's working very well.

Without doubt, the twenty-first century is the best time to be a consumer: choice, quality and value go way beyond anything we've had before, but this makes it a terribly hard time to be in business. Retailers are finding it difficult to sell us new products. Our homes are so crammed full of technology that there's nothing we really need to buy. Burglary is in decline as the resale value of previously lucrative items such as DVD players plummets. In 2004, DSG international plc (Dixons Stores Group) identified plasma-screen TVs as the triple-A "must-have" product for Christmas. They hardly sold any at all, as the seasonal shopping spree, which has been happening later and later since the turn of the century, finally decided not to bother happening at all.

The future for print media is far from bright. Sales of newspapers and magazines are in long-term and for many publications terminal decline; and while many publishers have been quick to develop online publishing strategies, fewer have managed successfully to develop online revenue models. Broadcasting is also suffering from the digital diaspora. Many cable and satellite channels are struggling to survive on advertising revenues alone, but at least they are doing better than digital radio channels.

On the web it's a similar story. Please indulge me while I slip into new economy-speak, but many businesses are failing to monetize their audiences in a fiercely competitive environment. Margins are low, there is no more low-hanging fruit and by and large, land-grab strategies result in little more than rapidly burning through your seed capital. The last major e-tailer to launch was Opodo in 2001. Visit a venture capitalist today and tell him you want to set up a dot.com business: you wouldn't get any more laughs if you turned up in a clown suit.

This is all bad news for the message pushers: the marketers, advertising executives and PRs. The fragmentation of the media landscape means that audiences are harder and more expensive to reach than ever. To illustrate, let us briefly rewind to 1988 and the dawn of my career. Back then "the media" meant four TV channels, a buoyant national press, a small number of specialist magazines and a handful of radio stations. It was easy to decide where all your advertising and PR budget should be spent. Today, not only is the audience difficult to reach, but it's also very good at ignoring advertising.

The media exists to deliver an audience to its advertisers. You might not like it – especially if you happen to be a journalist – but it's true. (The exception of course is the BBC, which many people in broadcasting believe exists simply to piss off those who are trying to deliver an audience to their advertisers.) By today's standards, achieving 10 million viewers for a terrestrial TV show is a phenomenal performance. Digital recording technology means that viewers can record what they like and watch it when they like; they can even opt to lose the adverts. Research into modern viewing habits shows that viewers in general, but males especially, are more likely to use their remote control to snack on three or four programmes simultaneously than to watch an entire programme in one sitting. A viewer might sit down to watch Premiership football on Sky, but as soon as the ball goes out for a throw in, it's over to MTV for a quick video, pausing to see what gives on Men and Motors then off to the Cartoon Network to see if *Dexter's Laboratory* is on, before flipping back to the football in time for the replay of the goal they've missed.

There is also a great deal of empirical evidence to suggest that advertising is not actually an effective way to communicate a message at all. From the mid-1990s up until the turn of the century, countless dot.com businesses launched, usually with millions of pounds of seed capital, on the back of a business plan built on advertising: selling "page impressions" ("eyeballs" looking at your advertisement, or hits on a website) and a bit of e-commerce. I worked at one of them. The popular rallying call at the time was "e-business or no business", and the column inches dedicated to the businesses of the future such as Baltimore, Clickmango, Lastminute.com, Soccernet, Premium TV, Razorfish, 365 Corporation and Boo.com, were incredible. As rallying calls go, "e-business and no business" might have been more appropriate, but this isn't a book about the era of dot.com failure. What is of interest is what happened to the market for page impressions. Back in 1998, 1,000 page impressions cost £35. Today, they can be bought for as little as a fiver. Websites struggle to sell their inventory of impressions and unless your site is a sprawling behemoth, you're not going to retire to a sandy beach on the back of any profits. The problem isn't that banner ads were necessarily a bad way of advertising, it's that their effectiveness was too easy to monitor. You could see how many people were responding to your call to action by simply counting the number of click-throughs – invariably a miniscule fraction of number of impressions.

This begs the question: how effective are the less accountable forms of advertising, such as print or TV ads? Inexpensive technology exists for printed publications to track the effectiveness of adverts carried within their pages. The inventor believed that this could be a very powerful tool, allowing publishers to demonstrate the true impact and value of advertising to their clients. So why is no publisher signing up for this system? If you read a paper today, can you actually remember one of the adverts that was in it? Well done. Now, can you remember ten? Thought not.

"How many people are taking any notice of our advertising?" it seems, is a question to which no one is especially keen to find the answer. It's not so hard to understand; just as turkeys wouldn't vote for Christmas, the advertising industry is unlikely to present a report to its clients entitled: "Why What You've Just Paid Us for Was a Complete Waste of Time". Even if you do get the punters to notice your ad campaign, it doesn't necessarily mean that your message is getting through. Today we regularly process well over 10,000 words or units of information each day. It is possible to watch TV, read a map, talk on the phone and drive a car all at the same time (although not strictly legal). With all this information available, it is unsurprising that there is such a struggle for mind share. In a recent survey carried out on behalf of the media corporation Emap, 85% of people who had seen the latest Orange TV campaign didn't know what the adverts were trying to tell them.*

So here we are: there are more money, more jobs and more people in the communications sector than ever before, while success is becoming a rarer and rarer commodity. It might sound grim, but it isn't. With success so difficult to achieve, most companies will settle for failure. It is possible to have a successful career without ever having to be involved in a successful project ever, and that is what thousands of people out there are doing. You could be one of them. It's never been a better time to fail. The mediocre have inherited the (business) earth. This culture has allowed City Slackers to proliferate in the communications and media sector and the impact that they are having on the economy, if not the organizations they work for, is enormous.

Earlier this year we decided to get our bathroom tiled. A two-day job, but we had to wait six months before the tiler could find the free time to come out and do it. Last week my agency advertised for a junior PR assistant. We had 165 applications.

---

*Source: EMAP 2000 Branding Conference DVD: Branding and Media Planners, McKevitt and Kenwood Limited, September 2004.

2 | **Buy Me!**

The most striking thing about our economic landscape is that it is geared up not to reward success, but to reward failure. "The exit strategy" is the salient issue for today's business leaders: this means that companies are driven by the issue of "how do I get my money out?"

This rationale has created a corporate culture that rewards image over substance: many successful careers are being built not on competence, but on an individual's ability to market him or herself successfully. To succeed you don't have to do your job: in many cases it's better not to, you just have to look like you're doing your job. And if you can make it appear that you're doing it well, all the better. This is obviously a much easier option, which is why so many people are doing it.

It's inevitable that some will misconstrue this central argument – through misunderstanding or mischief – but in an attempt to mitigate the inevitable brickbat I'd like to make the following point in big neon letters: not everyone who works in the communications and media sector is a City Slacker and not every City Slacker works in the communications and media sector.

For the record, I think that this sector attracts some of the most dynamic, interesting and creative minds in the world today. And I think you don't have to look hard to find talented people, with great ideas, who make a difference and who are prepared to put their neck on the line if that's what it takes to make the right decision that will move the organization forwards. These people have always worked in, and been attracted by, the sector and will continue to do so.

But now that the sector has become more bloated, and the tasks that it is charged with have become more difficult to solve, there are plenty of people coasting through their careers without actually having to contribute, let alone trying to contribute anything. The problem for businesses is that the City Slacker is virtually indistinguishable from a conscientious employee in a similar position. Moreover, the art of being a successful City Slacker requires relentless mendacity, so it should come as no surprise that many slackers are in denial about the real motivation behind their working practices. So, if you are reading about work in PR, marketing, advertising, sales or the media – to paraphrase Carly Simon – you probably think this book isn't about you. This will come as a shock – it might be!

How do you spot a City Slacker? It's not easy. In the olden days you had to be good to get to the top, everyone knew that. Careers were built upon success: product innovations, successful marketing campaigns, finding a gap or niche in a sector and launching into it. People had clearly defined responsibility and they were accountable. The move from corporate hierarchical structures to more flexible project teams and outsourcing services to third parties has brought with it a world of ambiguity. Audit any medium-sized organization today, and you will quickly find a surprising number of people who command a great deal of authority but no have genuine accountability for anything. The edges have been blurred and as a result nobody is quite sure where the buck stops.

For City Slackers, this is a very good thing. The moment the City Slacker actually starts doing the job, they run the risk of exposure. In a society where presentation is everything it's no longer about what you do, it's about how you *look* like you're doing it. Take every opportunity to ensure you are seen to be doing the job. The new breed of urban professionals might appear to be the ultimate "yes men": never challenging superiors, always putting the company first, but be on your guard – they will be cleverly undermining the boss because promotion can't come soon enough, and because it literally pays a City Slacker to keep moving. They will be armed with all the latest industry buzzwords, which will be rotated regularly to make them look well informed. The City Slacker is big on "strategic realignment", "corporate rebranding" and "brand repositioning" – anything with "re" at the front is good, it means they don't have to innovate. You will usually find mature versions "up to their neck" in a soft project with high visibility and no real chance of evaluation, for example, leading a team charged with redesigning the company's logo. This is a highly visible project which will elicit a strong emotional response internally, but will have zero impact on the performance (for good or ill) of the business. For the slacker, this is perfect.

Many companies will believe that a City Slacker is their biggest asset: a rising star who's never put a foot wrong, but the truth is that they never will have delivered anything. They might be big on the conference and networking scene, but that's because they're looking for their next gig. You will find City Slackers appearing regularly in the pages of your trade press, but that's probably because they've charged the company's PR agency with boosting their own profile, rather than the CEO's – who will be oblivious to this and simply lap up the great coverage.

A City Slacker is always busy. Everything about them will seem to have a sense of urgency: holding folders wherever they go, always on the mobile yet, ironically, virtually impossible to get hold of because they're always in meetings. If you work alongside one, you will find they are a great source of ideas for your project: the kind of person you can expect to send you an email outlining a few "blue-sky" ideas at 11 at night or slap in the middle of the weekend. You know they are always thinking about the company, even when they're asleep.

The reality is very different. The folders are no more than a prop; the mobile calls will be mostly personal, but they may concern the organization of an out-of-hours social event or may even be some "consultancy" for a competitor. Those great ideas, as we will see later, will be carried out at your own risk, to be immediately reclaimed in the unlikely event that they succeed (usually by sending a congratulatory email to you that is copied to the boss with the initial idea attached to the bottom as evidence). Those late-night emails are most probably the result of a few subtle changes to his internal PC clock and mail client set-up, courtesy of a helpful soul in the IT department.

The City Slacker carries files home every night. They are never opened. In fact, the best slackers never do any work at all – that's what agencies, freelancers and trainees are for. They'll always take the credit though, and the fact that they aren't doing any work explains why they seem to cope with stress so well.

City Slackers love jobs with grand-sounding titles. Invariably, these will bring a "What does that mean?" from family and friends. "Product manager" or "brand manager" are popular career choices for slackers, but the more nebulous the better: "product marketing executive/manager/ director", "marketing strategist", "head of brand development", "head of marketing communications EMEA" or "CRM strategy development manager".

Andy Fright was head of PR for a large entertainment corporation. The CEO asked him to put out a press statement announcing the appointment of a new marketing director at his company. Keen to make a good impression with the new boss, he immediately drafted a glowing press release, complete with the usual bogus quote about how much he was "relishing the fresh challenge at a new and exciting company" and submitted it to his incoming superior for approval. The release came back with only one amendment. The job title "marketing director" had been changed to "worldwide marketing director". Andy said that he felt like adding a paragraph saying the company was still looking for someone to handle marketing in outer space.

I should point out that City Slackers are not to be confused with good old-fashioned incompetents either. Slackers can be very striking individuals working for very impressive organizations. As Simon Bates was fond of saying during Radio 1's mawkish *Our Tune*, you have to read between the lines.

My first head-on collision with a classic City Slacker happened in 1999. Prior to this point, I'd been aware of their work but hadn't been unable to make any confirmed sightings. I went for a drink with an ex-colleague of mine, Guy Kingsley, who had joined a fledgling new media agency as publishing director. It was when he told me this story about the meeting he had just come from that I decided to start studying City Slackers in detail. After waiting longer than Greyfriars Bobby, Guy's agency had been granted preferred supplier status with one of the world's biggest mobile phone manufacturers. This was big news for him: an opportunity, he rightly felt, to grab a tight hold of the money tree and start shaking vigorously. Before he could get stuck into the project properly, the phone company's marketing director – a very amiable and capable chap – decided it would be useful if his brand manager paid a visit to give Guy and his team a handle on their "ongoing brand alignment and strategy".

On the day in question, Colin Levitt arrived – armed with laptop, PowerPoint presentation and firm handshake – to take them through his "strategic brand model". Looking back, his business card should have alerted Guy to the fact that he was about to witness something special. It read: "Head of Brand Alignment and Strategy EMEA", but the literally fantastic presentation still came as a real surprise. It would be so easy for Guy to claim that he was like the little boy who shouts out the truth in *The Emperor's New Clothes*, but it would also be a complete lie. He was taken in, just like everyone else.

The centrepiece of Colin's presentation was his "brand compass". This was a graphic image that, he informed Guy, had been beautifully realized by "one of the UK's leading design agencies" and was now being projected onto the boardroom wall. It was baffling, it was arcane and it was also a little bit scary. Clearly, "one of the UK's leading design agencies" had been heavily influenced by the work of Aleister Crowley. Guy wondered if his team were about to be initiated into the Masons and surreptitiously checked Colin's business card again to see if it carried any subheading like "Lord Grand High Wizard (MBA)". Guy showed me a hard copy of Colin's presentation in which he explained the arcane meaning of the brand compass. It was equally baffling and delivered in the manner of Alan Partridge's now infamous "World Cup Wall Chart", but I'll do my best to explain.

Colin's exposition was thus: each point on the compass represented a different brand within the company's family of brands. Each of these brands, in turn, corresponded to a different market demographic, which meant that the company was geared up to cater for every customer's "unique mobile device needs" as they progressed through various stages of their life. For example, at North was the "Chav" brand: a collection of cheap and decidedly miserable phones targeting "shell-suited youths on inner-city housing estates", while at South was the "Chi-Chi" brand and a set of chic, aesthetically pleasing handsets targeting "Prada-wearing mid-life to early-grey females".

At this point Guy looked around at his colleagues, hardworking and intelligent individuals one and all. They were, to a man, nodding sagely at everything Colin said. There was clearly much wisdom here, if only stupid old Guy could understand it. Guy tried very hard but quickly realized it was beyond him; he couldn't get his head around this strategy at all. The problem Guy had was that while Colin's company was a household name, he had never heard of any of his eight compass brands before and simply couldn't see how they could be made to resonate with consumers. People might say: "I've got a Nokia" or a Motorola or a Sony Ericsson, but beyond that ...? Guy also didn't think anyone would want the cheap, tatty phones at point North, whoever they were. In fact, he thought it more likely that the "shell-suited youths on inner-city housing estates" would want to get their hands on the high-value products being pushed to "Prada-wearing mid-life to early-grey females", perhaps even employing criminal tactics to achieve it.

In addition, it was difficult to see how you moved round the compass: from shell-suited youth to fat-arsed businessman, missing out super youth and mid-grey women on the way. And even if Guy was completely wrong and it really did work just as Colin had said, what had this brand compass actually told us? As far as he could see, nothing other than they were selling cheap phones to people who could only afford cheap phones and expensive ones to people with loads of money who were more likely to shop around. Guy thought he must be missing something. He wasn't.

His colleagues left the meeting thinking Colin was a genius. The company view was that Colin was smart and that he'd spotted something really clever. And they were concerned that their own response to this brief would seem unsubtle and too straightforward, rather like a child's drawing next to a Michelangelo. Guy's team spent countless hours on that account. At least the billing was good.

By now you'll probably have guessed that Colin's brand compass didn't work at all, but that isn't the point. Colin left the company about six months after his meeting with Guy. Having spent over two years putting together this strategy, but just a couple of months into its implementation, he decided it was time to take on a fresh and exciting new challenge somewhere else: somewhere the pay was better. Colin got himself a job as "head of strategic something or other" at one of the biggest telecoms network operators in Europe. He was actually headhunted *specifically* for the work he'd done in putting together this ludicrous, fundamentally flawed but ultimately unproven strategy. And fair play to him, you might say.

My outtake from this was that Colin had the perfect job. His company bought into his strategy because, having made phones for every market, the last thing they wanted to hear was: "You can't be all things to all people". With his "Oh yes we can" strategy, Colin was kicking against an open door. He'd spent two years as a "head of ..." which meant that his team had spent two years researching a brand strategy and developing a product suite against which there were absolutely no measures other than "we must have one". The brand compass was a very complicated way of saying: "We sell expensive phones to people who can afford them and cheap phones to people who can only afford *them*." Once he'd conceived his strategy, his job was simply to communicate – or, if you will, "evangelize" – it to the people who would be charged with delivering it: an army of product managers, agencies and marketing services providers – none of whom even reported to him. Colin had spent two years flying round EMEA (wherever that is) having the same meetings. In other words, he had a huge amount of authority and absolutely no accountability.

The project was an exercise in job self-creation. All the company wanted was some justification and reassurance for something that they were planning to do anyway. To come up with his idea might have taken five minutes, but Colin cleverly spread the work out over two years: commissioning research projects, organizing focus groups from third parties and having an awful lot of meetings. *

This is not an isolated case. If you want evidence, next time you go to your local multiscreen entertainment complex (or "cinema", as it was formerly known), take a close look at one of those big cardboard cut-outs advertising films that are coming soon. If it's a typical

---

*You might be interested to know that this wasn't Colin's only project. As a reward for his blood, sweat and tears – turning five minutes' work into an undeliverable strategy in just two years – the company let Colin look after some of its sponsorship deals: specifically those involving snowboarding and football. Colin liked snowboarding and football. Interestingly, his new company has just announced two sponsorship deals: with a snowboarding event and a football club.

blockbuster – one of those CGI-ridden monstrosities masquerading as high art – check out the small print along the bottom. In many cases you will notice a number of brands and logos on the standee: Coca-Cola, Levi's, Nike, BMW, Sony PlayStation, Microsoft Xbox, Nintendo, Electronic Arts, 7-Up, MGM, M&Ms, Eminem and God knows what else. Of course, this has been prevalent for many years; the cross-promotion of movies, CDs, video games and merchandise releases over the past decade has become a business in itself, but it is worth considering just how many thousands of people are now employed in this micro-industry.

The opportunity for City Slackers is enormous. For example, on a single item of packaging or point of sale material (PoS) often you can find almost a dozen brands competing with each other for miniscule space, positioning, hierarchy and association. Undoubtedly, each one will have a brand manager employed specifically to protect its own interests. How much time went into this, I wonder? How many PowerPoint presentations, meetings, pie charts, market maps, lunches, focus groups, market research, evaluations, approval processes, more lunches and more meetings? A long, drawn-out process indeed, to achieve the simple objective of making sure that the logo is in the right place along the bottom of a product that 99% of people will take no notice of whatsoever. In fact, you'll probably be the first person who's looked at it in detail.

Paranoia is rife within the brand industry: "Can we associate our product and brand with this?" "What do the focus groups think?" "Does the latest reality TV show winner have a face that will sell our sofas?" After deliberation and consultation with the market data, ultimately brand protectors will arrive at some startling conclusion: "Hmm... it's risky, but what about brand equity?" "Can it sustain the association over the long term? Is it going to damage us? I know, let's have a meeting and a coffee to discuss it. Oh, and don't forget the PowerPoint so we can show somebody we're doing something."

And therein lies the problem. Companies and corporations the world over are so obsessed with preserving and exploiting their brand that a competitive culture has now emerged. So much time, energy and money is being disproportionately directed towards maintaining imagined "brand values" that the real issue is being masked: ultimately, it is only the quality of the product that the customer is interested in.

The zeitgeist has allowed quality control to go out of the window, marketing campaigns fudge the lack of real creativity and innovation, hence the current abundance of brain-numbing non-entities and "me-too" products flooding the marketplace. Most product launches fail. It's a fact. In the games industry, approximately 50% of sales come from just 10% of releases; similarly, the music industry is concentrating on fewer and fewer acts; having run out of recipes, confectioners are bringing out bigger/smaller/special edition versions of 60-year-old snacks. Companies have become so consumer-obsessed that brand managers and marketers are now having the times of their lives.

And who is benefiting from the rise in pseudo-science? Look round your office – are there more people in marketing positions that didn't exist three years ago and are you selling more as a result? The truth is that a brand-competitive culture is covering up for the inadequacies of the glut of poor, insipid and uninspired product. But this failure offers rich pickings for the City Slacker. The impact of all this effort is so slight, so marginal, that the individuals embroiled within it are unlikely to find that their performance (or lack of it) makes one iota of difference to the performance of the company.

The question "What makes a good brand manager?" is very difficult to answer, because the role is nebulous and ephemeral. And if you don't know what they are supposed to be doing, how do you know whether they're doing it well or not? The answer is that you don't, so any brand manager looking to move on will have to find another way of proving his worth to the business. This is how the City Slacker begins. The more effort they put into proving their own value, so it follows, the less time they have to spend doing the job. The objectives of the individual and the company are out of sync.

This situation is not exclusive to those who work in brand or product marketing. Across entire disciplines – marketing, sales, technology, PR, journalism, senior management, consultancy – the disconnect between companies and their employees has created the perfect environment for value avoidance. Today's generation of bright young things entering the workplace know what they want: more money, interesting careers, kudos and share options. Contestants on reality TV shows are widely and reasonably lambasted for openly admitting that they "want to be famous" without ever stopping to consider what it is that they want to be famous for. Similarly, the City Slacker wants the trappings of success without ever considering what they should get those trappings for.

In a popular series that recently showed on TV called *Dragons' Den*, budding entrepreneurs are invited to present their business ideas to a panel of super-wealthy businesspeople in the hope of receiving investment. More often than not all they receive is abuse, which does make for some interesting television. In a recent episode, a budding managing director pitched her idea to the "dragons". The idea itself was irrelevant – something to do with selling suits to businesswomen – but what was interesting was her personal circumstances and her view of them. Under cross-examination it transpired that previously she had been buying director at a major high-street retailer but was made redundant (not "fired", of course) and had set up her business as a consequence. The woman had a very high opinion of herself, needing the investment because, as a former director, "I don't come cheap". She needed to earn a minimum of £75,000 per year (more than three times the national average), regardless of the fact that her business was turning over a fraction of that.

Had I been a dragon, my advice would have been: "Well, work harder or get yourself another job as buying director, then." Live by capitalism, die by capitalism, because her "market value" is no more than what someone else is prepared to pay for it. She is not the exception.

People do believe they are worth what they are paid, most think they are worth more. And why shouldn't they? In the UK, CEOs earn on average 24 times as much as those on the shop floor – the biggest salary gap in Europe. In the US, CEOs earn on average 411 times more than those on the shop floor. The higher up the corporate ladder you go, the bigger the discrepancy between value and earnings. City Slackers recognize this: the higher up an organization you go, the more money you earn and the less you have to do. And as we will see, the higher up you go, the bigger the direct rewards for failure will become. Get fired (sorry, "made redundant") as a CEO and you won't need to work ever again. Play your cards right and you might not have had to do much work before you got there. City slacking is not the preserve of middle managers: everybody's at it.

Getting on is about marketing yourself effectively. Start by creating awareness about yourself and your capability, and make yourself famous within the organization with your diligent work ethic and achievements (perceived rather than actual, naturally). By cultivating an image as a real team player you will be surprised how eager others will be for you to succeed, and it won't be long before you're being considered for promotion or being offered more money to work elsewhere. This happens all the time. Given that so much of being a City Slacker involves marketing, it is perhaps appropriate that the role we are going to look at first is that of the marketer, and the product world in which they live.

3 | **Groundhog Day**

No one is sure who coined the phrase "the information age"*. It was first used probably in the late 1980s but it became common currency in the English language around 1990. Whoever it was could not have possibly imagined the impact that information technology would have on the world today: not just the impact of the "information superhighway"†, but advances in computing power, mobile communications, the massive effect of desktop publishing on print media and the explosion in the number of TV and radio channels.

Today it's not so much the information age as the information world. Modern consumers are bombarded with information. A typical issue of the *Sunday Times* contains more information than the average citizen of seventeenth-century England encountered in a lifetime. Never before have we had so much information on which to base our decisions, and we don't have to go all the way back to the seventeenth century to see how different things were.

To illustrate this, let's go back to 1979 and the arrival in Number 10 of Margaret Thatcher, leader of a new kind of Conservative government. I was 11 and, with my glorious failure as a tiler still five years ahead, making the best of life as a new entrant to the local comprehensive school, making

---

*Except for former US vice-president Al Gore, who claims he did!

† Also Gore, according to him and no one else.

new friends and opening my eyes to new experiences. But it wasn't all bad. At about this time, my cousin introduced me to the musical style known as heavy rock. He played a song by Led Zeppelin called *Custard Pie* (the opening track of the album *Physical Graffiti*). It sounded like nothing I'd ever heard before. (Breadth of experience context: that is to say, everything from *Top of the Pops* on TV through to the *Top 40* with Dave Lee Travis on Radio 1 – i.e. not that much, really). I was hooked. I saved up my pocket money and a few weeks later sent my dad on a mission to buy me the Led Zeppelin album. I had no idea what it was called but described the cover. Dad, clearly working out of his comfort zone, arrived home with the wrong album – but a great one nonetheless – the untitled album often referred to as *Led Zeppelin IV*, arguably their finest.

The album is still one of my favourites. But it wasn't without its problems for an 11-year-old now determined to become the biggest Led Zep fan in Christendom. For a kick-off, I knew nothing about them. The album sleeve was a useless source of information: no photos, no sleeve notes, nothing. The album didn't even have a title and the band's name didn't appear anywhere on the sleeve or the record. In fact, there was nothing to say this was Led Zeppelin at all. A few moments of doubt were only assuaged by dad's insistence that he had checked with the shop assistant before buying it. I weighed up the pitiful evidence and drew some conclusions: that the band was obviously American, and that "Led Zeppelin" must be the exotic name of the lead singer.

My efforts to find more information came to nothing. The 1970s version of the internet – my dad, a committed Neil Diamond fan – didn't know anything about them. They never appeared on *Top of the Pops*, nor on Dave Lee Travis's *Top 40* countdown. There was nothing about them in the *Daily Mirror*, and the three TV channels could be ruled out instantly. After several weeks' painstaking research I had amassed the following information from the only source available (friends and their older brothers).

1. Led Zeppelin were English.
2. They had made more than four albums.
3. There were four people in the band, two of whom were called Jimmy Page and Robert Plant.
4. Some, but by no means all, of their other albums could be found in some, but by no means all, record shops.
5. One of my mates, Matthew Forshaw, had one of their albums in his possession: *Led Zeppelin II*.

That was it. There were no books to buy. I even gave the *New Musical Express* (*NME*) a try, but although in turn it too became a fantastic discovery, it only seemed to cover punk and new wave bands.

The point is this: in 1979, Led Zeppelin was the biggest band in the world, but although they had sold more than 70 million albums in less than ten years, as far as most people were concerned, they might as well have been invisible. Type the words "Led Zeppelin" into Google today and you will be rewarded with over 750,000 pages. Budding Led Zeppelin fans could spend years trawling through that lot;

there's virtually nothing about them you couldn't find out, even Jimmy Page's shoe size*. If you prefer to take in your information off-screen, you could treat yourself to one of the 146 books about Led Zeppelin currently in print, and if you just want to listen to the music there are 151 separate music, video or DVD products available – not bad for a band that recorded their eighth and final studio album in 1978. Despite splitting up due to the death of their drummer, John Bonham, in 1980, Led Zeppelin is now featured on TV and radio more than ever before. (As I write this, in a quirk of synchronicity, they are being played on the digital radio channel that I'm listening to.)

This goes to illustrate an often unnoticed consequence of this data explosion: the world today is not only full of information, it is full of product. Product is the dominant feature of modern life. There are products for every conceivable purpose and several inconceivable ones. Products to save you time, pass the time, fill in the time you've saved, make life better, make other people's lives worse. There seems to be a product for everything. Back in 1899 the US Commissioner of Patent, Charles Duell, made one of the most famous gaffes of all time when he publicly stated: "Everything that can be invented, has been invented." Charles may have underestimated spectacularly the human race's capacity for invention, but his comment must surely strike a chord with modern consumers who, more affluent than at any time in history, are ceaselessly persuaded, cajoled and begged to spend their money on any

*Seven-and-a-half.

multitude of commodities designed to assuage a previously unrecognized need. The world is full of useless things.

As 3G-phone licensees and dot.com bankrupts will almost certainly attest, there is nothing more difficult to sell than the future. For example, approximately 85% of all new products launched into the grocery and allied trade sectors fail in their first year. This means that repackaging the past can be far more lucrative and much less risky. The more things change, the more they stay the same.

When marketing types are engaged in an activity or pursuit they find boring, they will often chuckle and employ the cliché "It's like selling soap powder!" to the general mirth of all within earshot. In many ways, soap powder presents the marketer with the ultimate challenge. Essentially, all they are selling is white – or occasionally blue – powder in a brightly coloured box that gets your clothes more or less as clean as the stuff in the next packet on the shelf. The weary search by these brands for a point of differentiation has similarities to the Cold War arms race pursued by Washington and Moscow: each side gamely attempting to get the edge over the competition for a brief period of time before their strategy is countered and the status quo is returned at a slightly higher entry price than before.

Television advertising in Britain began on 22 September 1955, and during its formative years the medium was dominated by soap powder manufacturers. The early commercials were very different from those with which we are familiar today: much longer and amusingly stilted, due to the relentlessly white middle-class values playing out the message with toe-curling slowness. The first adverts were simply adaptations of posters, flyers or newspaper ads with dancers and acrobats in different shades of white, while the announcer reassured viewers that "Persil washes whiter. That means cleaner". But the gloves were now off. For the next few years, battle royal waged on who was whiter:

Persil washes whiter.
Tide washes whiter still.
Surf gives me a bluey-whiteness I want from my wash.
OMO washes whiter than white.

By the 1970s the warfare had became literally biological, as enzymes were added to tackle the stains we couldn't see:

Bold: gets your clothes cleaner, because it's biological.
Ariel: hard on germs but kind to clothes.
Fairy: not just nearly clean, but really clean.

And just when we thought we were safe – whiter than white and germ-free – along came the neutron bomb of the detergent world: Radion Automatic. Radion moved the goalposts yet again: yes, we're clean and yes, we are whiter than white, but haven't you noticed how bad we smell?

Today, soap powder doesn't have to be a powder; it can be a liquid or tablet, it can get to the heart of your wash in a ball, it can be colour-friendly, non-biological or even eco-friendly. The net result of these changes is that the world has stayed exactly the same. Should people who wash their clothes in Surf be considered any more or less clean than people who use Ariel Ultra? Of course not. If clothes feels cleaner than they did 20 years ago, it's not something that anyone has noticed.

Commentators agree that the confectionery industry reached its nadir with the 1996 launch of Cadbury's Fuse bar. The Fuse, as its name implied, consisted of a selection of Cadbury classics – Crunchie, Boost, Caramel, etc. – fused together in one disappointing stick. It may have been, as Cadbury's company website maintains: "a response to a market demand for a more chocolatey snack" but it was unlikely to change the world, a long way away from the halcyon launches of Twix or KitKat some 50 years or so earlier.

The Fuse bar was taken as confirmation that the things-to-do-with-chocolate well had run dry. Despite selling 40 million bars in the first week thanks to a heavyweight advertising campaign, Fuse was never destined to trouble the heavyweights playing at the top of the chocolate premier league, fast establishing itself as nobody's favourite snack. Rather than give up on product development altogether, Cadbury and the other confectionery manufacturers did a very interesting thing: they began repackaging and reinventing existing brands. Mars Bar Dark, KitKat Chunky, Kingsize Snickers, Giant Smarties, limited-edition Lime KitKat. Cadbury even scrapped long-established brands such as Caramel and Wispa and reissued them as extensions of its flagship brand, Dairy Milk.

And as a result of all these changes, the world is exactly the same*.

---

*Except when you fancy a Wispa these days you have to ask for something called a Dairy Milk Bubbly. Genius!

In the 1994 film *Groundhog Day*, Bill Murray plays a washed-up weatherman who is condemned to relive the same day over and over again; every minute of his existence becomes a predictable series of events that he is unable to influence. It is a situation that many people working in marketing today must find familiar: the endless repetition of exactly the same processes to launch and promote seemingly indistinguishable products.

Cadbury's corporate website contains a very proud case study of the launch of the Fuse bar. Presented in the way that case studies always are, with the benefit of 20/20 hindsight, the truth is an inevitable victim. This makes it easy for the reader to see exactly why the product was such a rip-roaring success: because marketing is a science that is practised by wise men and women. The case study spells out the recipe for successful product launches, completely free of charge. All you have to do is to follow this foolproof process, and you too could have a winner like Fuse in your hands.

1. Find a market using market research.
2. Develop a product.
3. Test the product out on focus groups.
4. Spend loads on packaging and advertising. (NB: Take care to ensure that you make this exercise sound as scientific as possible. Under no circumstances must you imply that you chose the packaging because you liked the colour best or thought the creative was funny. Use phases like "the advertising focus-grouped well".)
5. Repeat for next product.

Success really couldn't be any simpler, could it? And indeed this template is a standard used to develop products in a variety of industries and sectors, not just confectionery. There's only one tiny flaw with this process: the vast majority created by it fail spectacularly.

In the retail and grocery trade, 85% of products fail in the first year. In the music industry, where historically the business strategy has been "if you throw enough shit at a wall, some of it will stick", something in the order of 80 to 90% of new releases will fail, meaning that you're going to be doing a lot of throwing. In the video games industry, 10% of titles released account for 50% of all sales, which means that most products fail to recoup their development costs. In magazine publishing more than 80% of new launches close within 12 issues, while in book publishing the situation's even worse, with a tiny proportion of new releases accounting for the majority of sales. In fact it's so bad, the chances are you won't be actually reading this book. And if you bought it in the remaindered section of "Books Books Books", it only goes to show that being right has nothing to do with being popular.

We can see that there is nothing new to say about chocolate or soap powder, but it's worse than that: there's nothing new to say about Led Zeppelin, Coca-Cola, Levi's or Sony PlayStation, either. The joy for the City Slacker is that if they're moderately careful they can coast through project after project, safe in the knowledge that if they manage to achieve a modest one-in-eight success rate, they'll still outperform most of their contemporaries in product marketing. The City Slacker quickly realizes that all they have to do is to breeze through the process on autopilot, taking care to look as busy as possible in the process and deliver failure after failure. No one will be expecting success anyway.

The long-term outlook for the City Slacker looks brighter still, because the great news is that most corporate organizations believe that there's no substitute for experience. The business world is always on the lookout for people with experience. So, once you've managed to get a few failures under your belt, people will really start to believe in you. You'll be learning from experience, and that experience is the most valuable commodity you have to sell. It is experience that will get you a promotion, land you a pay rise or help you clinch that killer job. You may find yourself headhunted, and even if you're not targeted for promotion there will be another company out there that will be delighted to have an individual of your experience on the team. And what about ability? I'm afraid no one cares. Einstein would struggle to get a job leading a modern research team, his CV wouldn't stack up: "It's clear young Albert's not short of ability, but he's been working as a patent's clerk, for goodness sake – where's his experience?"

Experience is the biggest red herring of them all. The people who make a difference in organizations are those with ability, regardless of their experience. However, the ones with experience are far more likely to get promoted. Despite the propaganda from business schools, management consultants and the people doing these jobs already, most marketing positions are neither difficult nor difficult to understand, and many people perform well in these positions without any formal training. Twelve months into any product marketing position and the City Slacker, realizing that they have absolutely no control over the success or failure of their product whatsoever, will be able to do the job standing on their head.

Working in marketing at a record company?

1. Get the product reviewed: not you personally – your PR agency.
2. Get the record played on radio: not you personally – the record plugger.
3. Get some good packaging together, some PoS and a decent video: not you – the design company and video director.
4. Now sit back, enjoy the launch party, wait for the record to fail and drop the band.
5. Repeat.

Working for a video games company? Even easier.

1. It's probably the latest version of a franchise (say *Tomb Raider 7* or *FIFA Soccer 06*), so all you have to do is exactly the same as you did last time with a few minor changes. For example, getting a new model to play Lara Croft or the latest star footballer to appear on the packaging.
2. Repeat.

Working for a regional radio station?

1. Check the audience figures.
2. Run a promotion that involves the listeners

(search for Radio Yawn's worst karaoke singer, for example).

3. Check the figures again. If they go up, take the credit. If they go down, blame macro factors but commission some research to show how, as a result of your promotion, the listeners now think more highly of the brand and claim a "qualitative rather than a quantitative" improvement.

4. Repeat.

Working for a soft drink manufacturer?

1. Look at the music charts, see who's popular and sponsor them.

2. Get them to appear in some ludicrously expensive adverts.

3. Spend as much as possible and when presenting the results – which invariably will be that lots of people saw your ads and like the performer – drop in a few anecdotes about how much the campaign annoyed the folks working for "The Red Devil of Atlanta City".

4. Repeat.

This is not simplistic or far-fetched: this is what really happens. If it's difficult to do something new now, just think how hard it's going to be next year and the year after that. And the year after that. If your strategy is to launch your new cars in increasingly exotic locations, how long is it going to be before you have to start thinking about taking the reviewers to the Moon or Mars? How lavish can your opening night party be? Do you attempt to reanimate John Lennon or Elvis as part of the live entertainment?

When there's nothing to say, maybe it is best to say nothing. There are a lot of people organizing launches for the new BMW 5 Series or the Ford Ka, but sooner or later someone is going to realize that just dropping the keys off at the magazine's office will have pretty much the same effect. That day, when it comes, will be a dark day for the City Slacker.

In 2001 I was fortunate to attend the UEFA Cup final in Dortmund between Spain's Alavés and Liverpool. It was a thrilling match which Liverpool won 5–4 in front of a TV audience of approximately 160 million people.

A few weeks before the final, Motorola announced that they had completed a multi-million pound sponsorship deal with UEFA. A few weeks before that announcement, Motorola had shut down factories in Scotland and Ireland. Reports varied but an estimated 3,000 people lost their jobs due to abysmal handset sales* (now, if only *they'd* had a brand compass).

The UEFA Cup Final was Motorola's first match of the deal and as a result they had an exclusive slot on every single advertising hoarding around the ground. Blanket coverage in fact: a fantastic opportunity to push a new message to tens of millions. And their response to this opportunity? To have the word *Motorola* printed on every single hoarding.

---

*Source: bbc.co.uk, 24.04.01 ("Motorola to close Scottish plant").

How many people, I wondered, would go out the next day and buy a Motorola mobile phone as a result of this activity? How many people would be "more aware" of Motorola than they were before the exercise? And how many would think, as I did, why is the company that has just sacked 3,000 people spending millions to print the word *Motorola* on 100 advertising hoardings?

For the City Slacker marketer, the information and product boom has been a win–win situation. More marketing pounds to spend, more product to shift (or fail to) and more "busy work" to be done. Best of all, nobody's expecting you to have any kind of success at all, let alone get things right every time. The pay-off is a culture where failure is accepted as inevitable, as we cycle through ever-decreasing circles of brand extensions, fresheners and relaunches.

It should come as no surprise that on average, brand or product managers stay in the same job for an average of just 18 months. Three months to settle in, nine months to do the job – failing, remember, more than eight times out of ten – and six months to find another position.

The way that companies recruit supports the City Slacker culture. As we've seen, recruiters and CVs focus on experience not ability, and certainly not success. Candidates with blue chip names on their CV will find their cachet increased with prospective employers. Interviewees provide a post-rationalized version of their career, evidencing decisions with hindsight. Interviewers will base their decision based on the candidate's ability to do the job, from evidence gained at the interview (a breeze for any experienced City Slacker) and their weight of relevant experience. Sometimes companies will use supporting evidence from some meaningless aptitude or psychometric tests. References – always available upon request – will be provided by individuals nominated by the candidate and will invariably provide a positive endorsement of their capabilities.

Every new appointment is risky. There isn't an organization in the world which can say that every employee has gone on to make a positive contribution to the business – the very opposite is often closer to the truth. An applicant with ability and a genuine track record for success will be almost impossible to single out because this process provides the perfect cover for City Slackers, who will be better camouflaged than a leopard in a leopardskin coat factory.

Patrick Carney works for a London PR agency that operates for hi-technology clients. A few years ago, just as the internet was establishing itself as a serious channel, he was representing an American software company that specialized in CD-ROM encyclopaedias. Clearly, this was a company that felt threatened by the growth of the web, and in order to square the circle they seconded their vice-president of marketing, the improbably named Jahan Shue from their head office in San Diego, to London with a view to establishing some strategic partnerships. Naturally, Jahan needed a place to work from and Patrick was happy to offer his client the use of a desk, PC, meeting room and telephone. Back in San Diego, Jahan's weekly contact reports were going down a storm. He had an MBA from Yale and as far as his paymasters were concerned he was doing a tremendous job, strategizing the route to market in Europe, providing them with cutting-edge information about the nuances of the emerging online market, identifying threats and opportunities.

In reality Jahan was just doing desk research, obviously mindful of the fact that his US colleagues were not party to the relevant European trade press that he was cutting and pasting into his reports, which told them exactly what they wanted to hear: that the product had real potential and that they were going to make a lot of money. Two months into the job, Jahan had several West End musicals under his belt but as yet had been unable to secure a single meeting, largely due to the fact he hadn't contacted anyone. The only meeting of any substance on the horizon was one that Patrick arranged: a meeting on Jahan's behalf with one of his other clients, a fledgling internet service provider (ISP) from Cambridge that went on to become Pipex.

As is the way with agencies, there can be a great deal of benefit in putting two clients together, and Patrick had pitched an opportunity to the ISP's marketing director that involved bundling a demo of Jahan's software with their internet access CD-ROM. The promotion would be of mutual benefit to both parties, giving the ISP some added value and, at the same time, putting Jahan's software in front of hundreds of thousands of potential customers, with negligible risks and costs for both parties. All in all, it sounded like a winner.

A meeting was held in Cambridge, which seemed to go pretty well. On the way back to the station Patrick asked Jahan how he felt the meeting had gone.

"I don't know what to think until I've spoken to the US," replied Jahan.

"Yeah, but how do you think it went?" Patrick asked him again.

"I don't know what to think until I've spoken to the States," repeated Jahan, with slight annoyance.

Undeterred, Patrick tried a slightly different tack: "Look, I know you've got to speak to the States, but you must have your own opinion about whether it's a good idea or not."

"Look," said Jahan sternly, "I don't know what to think. I'll speak to the States, find out how the land lies and then I'll know what to think!"

What Jahan realized was that making a recommendation would mean having to take ownership of a possibly incorrect decision. On his own in Europe, having a ball, the last thing he needed was to have his judgement called into question; so long as he stuck to the hypothetical, he was on safe ground. To go back and say: "I think we should do this," ran the risk of failure; much better to get someone else to make the decision and run with that. Not only would it give him something to do, but if it went wrong nobody would hold him responsible.

In the culture of failure, blurred responsibility and nebulous accountability are welcomed support mechanisms. They are used to mitigate individual performance when unsuccessful product launch follows yet another unsuccessful product launch. But these mechanisms are inherent, and what we will look at in the next chapter is the effect that they have on organizations on those rare occasions when things actually go right.

4 | **Success Has Many Parents, but Failure is an Orphan**

You might not know this – and I'm not one to blow my own trumpet – but a few years ago I came up with the idea for a revolutionary new concept: a technology that is having a massive additional impetus to the already rapidly expanding market for DVDs.

At the time I was employed as the product director of a technology business. Since I came up with the concept, my erstwhile employer has invested several million pounds in the technology's development and has taken the product successfully to market. The shareholders support their faith in my brilliant idea: the company announced that it had secured a worldwide patent and within 12 months its share price had increased by over 1000%. It has a market cap of £50 million, offices across Europe and the US and has won a seemingly endless list of business awards and plaudits. However, by the time the company had started reaping the rewards of my brilliant idea, I had long since exited the business.

You might be wondering why on earth they allowed such an obviously valuable employee like myself to leave at all. You might imagine that, as I tendered my resignation, my fellow board directors burst into tears, got down on their knees and begged me to stay, promising sacks full of cash and a company Ferrari. In fact, nothing could be further from the truth.

While I don't think they were actually happy to see me go (and indeed during the past twelve months they have become good clients of my new business), I am certain they didn't lose too much sleep over my decision to quit. The share price didn't plummet either (although, to be honest, at the time I left it didn't have very far to fall).

So, let me share with you the story of my departure and clear up this mystery of how a successful business was happy to part company with its creative genius once and for all.

My decision to resign was precipitated by events at MusicWorks 2002 – a music industry conference that is held annually in Glasgow (the location is crucial). The first thing to admit is that I wasn't acting alone. My partner in resignation was the company's marketing director James Austen who was and still is a close friend as well as a colleague.

It was little more than ten months since my brilliant concept had been presented to the board: the patent had been accepted, development of the software was well underway, and the first two products made using a prototype of the system were almost due for release. James had spotted a fantastic opportunity for the company to present its technology to a core market. According to the promotional bumph, the MusicWorks 2002 audience would attract all of the music industry's main movers and shakers. It was clear to us that all of these people would take just one look at what our technology had to offer and snap it up on the spot. Fortuitously, an old friend of mine was one of the organizers and he gave us a presentation slot for nothing (street value: £5,000).

An audience of such big-hitters required heavyweight representation. The rest of the board agreed with us – this was a great networking opportunity – and the product director and marketing director (James and I) were dispatched forthwith. We were confident of returning with, if not a multi-million pound deal, then at least a host of red hot leads. We spent the following days and nights polishing our presentation until it shone like a star.

Now, back to the Glasgow location. The thing is, Glasgow is fantastic city, but, as we were about to discover, it's a long way from London, which is where all the music industry people live. MusicWorks 2002 just happened to coincide with a Celtic v Rangers football match, and through an old contact James had managed to secure four free tickets in the best seats in the ground. This gave us a brilliant opportunity for some corporate entertaining: we could soften up the musical bigwigs at the footy before nailing them with our presentation the following morning. A fantastic plan.

Our suspicions about just how crucial attendance at MusicWorks 2002 was considered by the music industry were aroused when we started phoning around, extending our corporate hospitality to our music biz contacts. No one we knew was going; we literally couldn't give the tickets away. Still, both James and I are huge football fans so they didn't entirely go to waste. It would be a great way to relax and clear our heads before the big presentation (and neither of us had been to an old firm game before).

The deal was that I would do the presentation (after all, James had got the old firm tickets), James would field questions from our 200-strong audience, we'd bask in applause, swap business cards and start taking the orders.

Things started well. The venue was great, our run through was slick (the soundman told us) and our presentation looked great on the big screen. An entertaining game at Parkhead was followed by a spot of light drinking and an early night to ensure clear heads and sharp minds.

The alarm bells started ringing the next morning as we registered for the conference. Despite this being the second day, there were a huge number of unclaimed name badges on the reception desk, and while I didn't recognize the individual names, I did recognize all the companies. It appeared that the movers and shakers were planning on arriving unfashionably late – probably coming up for the afternoon, reasoned James, quite reasonably, giving them plenty of time to catch our presentation.

The opening programme was generally quite interesting, if largely irrelevant. As James and I were fans not only of football but also of arthouse cinema, we especially enjoyed the presentation by director Lynne Ramsey, whose latest film *Morven Caller* was premiering in the city that evening. We were surprised that there were so few people attending: there were no more than 50 people in the auditorium, and if the subject matter wasn't highly relevant to the music industry, when we'd first looked at the timetable, this really did seem to be a must-see presentation to us. We wondered if Lynne would be checking out our presentation. Probably not, reasoned James.

Perhaps more alarming than the low turnout, at least at this stage, was that as the day wore on it became clear I was losing my voice. I'd been suffering from a throat infection that had now passed but which had left me distinctly croaky; a condition that had not been helped by my enthusiastic support for "The Bhoys" the previous evening.

Despite a sensible taking-it-easy approach to the evening's entertainment, I woke that morning to find that my voice was going; by lunchtime, it had disappeared altogether. I could barely whisper, let alone talk, and delivering the presentation was going to be impossible. There was only one thing for it: a visibly concerned James would have to step into the breach.

We got into position early, sitting up on the stage in the large 200-seater auditorium, and nervously waited for the audience to arrive. "You'll be fine, James," I whispered, as we continued to wait. And wait. And wait. We should have started at 2.00pm and it was now five past. Clearly the previous session must have overrun, because there was still no sign of our audience. At ten past two, James went out to check the signage while I sipped yet another glass of warm water.

At quarter past, James returned and suggested that we just get on with it, so the presentation began. I am going to assume that you were not one of the 11 people in attendance when we finally kicked off at 2.20pm, and as such you'll probably want to know how it went. In style it was very much like *The Sooty Show* without puppets. James bumbled his way though an unfamiliar presentation with all the authority of a man who didn't really know what he was talking about, while I whispered in his ear and he paraphrased my responses for the benefit of the audience ("What's that, Steve? You want to play your xylophone!?!" – that kind of thing).

It was difficult to gauge which aspect was the more humiliating: our comic performance or the miniscule size of the attendance. The Question and Answer session (just one of each) was much shorter than anticipated and we wrapped up at about 2.55pm to the sound of one hand clapping. As we were packing up and getting ready to put the whole sorry experience behind us, one member of the audience pulled James to one side for a chat (no point doorstepping the mute, I supposed) and, after an animated and positive discussion, exchanged business cards. For a moment, I clung to the hope that this might not be a complete waste of time after all. Maybe this person was MD of Polydor who, noticing the poor attendance, had spotted that his company were ideally placed to sign us up and use our barnstorming technology to gain first-mover advantage in the fledgling DVD market. This could see us pluck victory from the jaws of defeat: the numbers didn't matter after all! Like I said, it was about quality not quantity. James returned.

"Who was that? Anyone interesting?" I whispered hopefully, laptop now safely packed away and ready to go to the next session.

"No. Just some bloke who wanted to know if we'd be interested in him doing a website for us."

James looked at his watch. "Fancy a pint?"

And with that, we left the MusicWorks 2002 Conference forever.

Over a demoralized pint, I hit James with my bombshell (which might have been more poignant had I not had to repeat it three times before he heard me).

"James, I can't do this anymore. I don't think I'm really cut out for this selling technology business if I'm being honest. The time has come to do something else. When we get back in tomorrow, I'm going to offer to resign."

James sipped his pint of heavy, pausing for a moment to reflect on the news that Musicworks 2002 was going to be my epiphany. "That's the best idea I've heard in ages," he said brightly, "So am I." And so it came to pass that less than 24 hours later both the product director and the marketing director had had their resignations gratefully accepted and had been made "an offer to leave".

I bet you can't believe that, can you? Just ten months after coming up with the concept that saved the company, they made no effort to stop me going. Where was the comforting arm around the shoulder, the reassuring voice telling me not to worry about being humiliated in front of 11 people? Where was the advice that greater things lay ahead? What short memories people have! Except, well … I'll come clean. It wasn't really all down to me.

What is true is that I had *proposed* the concept of creating interactive DVD titles to the board, but it wasn't all my idea. The original idea was born out of a brainstorming session between the company's two senior producers and myself. One of them had a concept for a game using audio CDs and this was developed to come up with a game that used video clips on DVD.

The concept would have remained on the drawing board had it not been for the support and vision of my MD, who immediately realized we were onto something.

Before taking things further he instructed James to research whether or not a market existed for such a product. James's team did a very thorough job and produced a robust piece of research to support the market opportunity. This opportunity would have remained theoretical, had it not been for the technical director who realized that while it was possible to create interactive titles, to do so was beyond the power of all the available DVD authoring systems. We would have to create our own authoring system, he explained, but by doing so we would be able to apply for a patent. We would then be able to license the technology to other companies so that they could make their own interactive content and titles. His team would conceive, design and develop the software.

Unfortunately, we didn't have enough money to finance the development. To raise the money to do this, the finance director and CEO would have to convince city investors that all of the above was the best way to spend their money; moreover, that the extra investment required would give them a huge return on their investment in the long run. I could go on and through all 90 people who worked in the business and all those who have passed through subsequently, all of whom will be able to claim compellingly all or part of some key milestone in the project's development and all of whom will undoubtedly highlight the technology in bold, 36-point lettering on their CV. By the same token, all of those 90 people (me included) will have exorcised from their CVs any involvement in the less profitable projects in which the business was involved.

This is not a criticism of my former employer at all: they survived by learning from these early setbacks and have gone on to establish a multi-million pound business in a market where few have survived at all. However, what their example illustrates is how City Slackers' successful careers can be built upon vicarious – rather than actual – success. The City Slacker knows that simply being seen in the right place at the right time is much more beneficial than doing a fantastic job in the wrong place at the wrong time. A brilliant performance in a doomed company will always be demanding and unrewarding; coasting along in a successful business is much, much easier and will make your CV shimmer and sparkle.

Companies rarely make major changes unless things are going wrong. Success is shared throughout the business. When a product succeeds, the whole company pats itself on the back. Product development always knew they were onto a winner; the marketing department delivered a brilliant campaign; the PR team made sure that all-important word of mouth started to happen in playgrounds and at water coolers while the sales team pulled up trees to get the order and make sure the thing was widely available in retail outlets. Beyond the company, the advertising, design, direct marketing, telesales and retail support agencies will be taking plaudits within the relevant trade press and, no doubt, adding a case study to their credentials. In short, everyone will be leveraging the success either to strengthen their personal position or to win more business.

While there's nothing intrinsically wrong with these no doubt uplifting but invariably smug displays of self-congratulation masquerading as team spirit, there is a pay-off. Whenever they begin to experience success, almost all companies become surprisingly tolerant of incompetence. Like a football manager, no executive wants to change a winning team. Maybe the marketing manager lacks imagination. So what? Look at the money we're making, where's the problem? Well, success inevitably means expansion, and like driftwood, over the course of a few short years that unimaginative marketing manager may have floated to a position of greater responsibility. They may even have a team of product managers working under them. Each one of these product managers will have been hired to ensure that the marketing manager has less actual work to do, which is good, because now the marketing manager has the freedom they need to spend all their available time "managing the team". Which, of course, they do with the same lack of imagination that they displayed in their original position.

Given just how tolerant of mediocrity we are, it's no surprise that most of the companies we work for are carrying more fat than an American tourist's sandals. Show me any profitable company employing more than 30 people and I'll show you a company that could lose at least 15% of its staff without affecting its performance. Were you to interview the staff, I'd guarantee that everyone would be able to identify one or two individuals whose role is a mystery to them.

Furthermore when, inevitably, the bad times happen and job cuts come, there will be no natural justice. The diligent account manager regularly working 14-hour days, who took just five days' maternity leave and won the company prize for best employee idea, will be emptying her desk alongside her City Slacker peer who regularly took two-hour lunches because they spent most of their time organizing the monthly "Payday Friday" night out. When they apply for another job, their relative performance will count for nothing. Both will submit CVs that have "account manager" written on them and both will have the opportunity to "interpret" their career history in whatever way they see fit. If the City Slacker performs at the interview – and they will – they will win again.

The corporate world is a landscape of hot-seat jobs. Marketing executive is a stepping-stone to product manager, which leads to brand manager, to marketing manager, to brand director, marketing director, group marketing director and to worldwide marketing director. It is not unusual to find a marketing director in his early 30s; they get there simply by making the right moves at the right time. There is a mad dash to get to the top as quickly as possible. Recently, I was in a meeting with a 53-year-old marketing manager. I had to stop myself from asking him what went wrong, as it has become such a junior position and unusual to find it filled by anyone over the age of 35. This was no slur on the man's marketing ability (although in truth he wasn't very good), but it was a major indictment of his inability to work his way up the corporate ladder.

Take the textbook example of a City Slacker extraordinaire called Colm Mahoney. Colm began his career in 1995 as the staff writer on a run-of-the-mill video games magazine. Over the next three years he had risen to the giddy heights of news editor and, obviously concerned by his lack of progress, decided to chance his arm elsewhere. The day he handed in his notice, his editor Allan Bragg invited me out for a pint to celebrate. Likeable though Colm was, his indolence was legendary and as Allan was much tougher than any of his previous editors, had he not resigned, almost certainly he would have been fired.

Colm did have a gift for comedy and down the pub he was a very funny guy, but he wasn't what you'd call a career man, so it was widely felt that in moving to become PR executive for a small software publisher, he was going to be punching well above his weight. As predicted, Colm took to his new job like a duck to cycling. He could be found every Friday morning at the office of his old employer – presumably "doing PR" – and after a few lunchtime shandies, he would disappear to his mum's for the weekend. To be fair, Colm was very open about his lack of application and would often refer to his "1973 Job"*. Six months later, Colm's life was transformed. The company he was working for was bought by a giant French publisher which was looking to set up a head office in the UK. By sheer luck, Colm found himself installed as "head of communications", a job whose function he described as "flying round Europe, having meetings. And wanking in hotel rooms".

Five years after leaving the magazine on probably not more £14,000 a year, Colm joined one of the biggest US

---

*A reference to the introduction of the three-day week by Conservative PM Ted Heath.

software publishers as European marketing director on over eight times that amount. When I bumped into him recently he was as affable as ever, laughing at his good fortune and perfectly candid about how unqualified he was for the job: "I know nothing about marketing," he admitted, "but my CEO thinks I'm brilliant because I'm the only marketing director who doesn't ask for more money to spend."

Don't make the mistake of thinking Colm is stupid. He knows full well that he can't do the job, but he's smart enough to know that by employing a good advertising agency and a half-decent PR agency he can look like he does. Colm gets away with it because his company is enjoying a good period of trading due to a strong product line-up. Its slate of quality titles and franchises will keep the profits rolling in for some time yet. The truth is, in fact, that its market is so clearly defined that the marketing doesn't make much difference. So Colm's job is safe and secure because nobody is going to be scrutinizing his performance when, evidently, the company is operating so well. It would be very difficult to do his job badly. There are times to take risks, but invariably it is never when things are going well. Why rock the boat? Keep your head down, look busy and you'll be fine. No, the time to take risks is when things are going wrong, when a maverick decision can be explained away as a considered but radical attempt to jump-start the business. You're probably going to lose your job whatever happens, so the best thing to do is to make as much noise as possible in the hope that someone will come to the rescue.

Sean Neal resigned from his position as brand director of an old school publisher that sold magazines in order to take a job as the marketing director for a new media company. Unlike his old company, which sold magazines for money, his new company gave all its content away free on the internet. The first three months were fantastic: a seemingly bottomless pit of seed capital, and a charismatic MD given to making impromptu speeches about how they were all building the future, made for an exciting, adrenaline-fuelled work environment. Every day new people were joining the business to start new projects as the company rapidly scaled up. Board meetings were held on beanbags, there was a pool table and Sony PlayStation in the office, music was on all the time, and although no one skateboarded through the office, one bloke did have a micro-scooter. Sean loved it. It would take a lot to tarnish the lustre of this anti-corporate media corporation, he thought.

And it did. Sean began to feel nervous when a meeting in the canteen with the company finance director revealed that, rather than the modest £10,000 per week they were aiming to turn over, the business was actually turning over less than £100 per week. Over the next few weeks, Sean thought he could detect a note of urgency creeping into the MD's impromptu speeches. It's a familiar story – the company went bust six months later – and not one we need to go into here, but what is interesting for us is the way in which Sean turned this crisis into an opportunity.

Sean realized that the revenue situation was an insurmountable problem, but rather than panic, he committed his entire marketing budget to a high-profile, highly visible and highly creative campaign that significantly raised awareness about his company's websites. Now, this might sound like a reasonable thing to do – and indeed to Sean's bosses it did – but more awareness was the last thing the company needed. The sites were already popular, generating plenty of traffic; the company's problem was that it was finding it impossible to engage this audience financially. They were happy to come and be entertained, but they weren't so interested in spending. For Sean, on the other hand, who needed to find himself a new job, it was an issue of raising both his own profile and the profile of his work. The campaign itself was memorable and he that ensured his PR agency grabbed every opportunity they could for him to appear in the trade press: columns, profile pieces, interviews.

With all the groundwork in place he was able to leverage his contacts at his advertising and media agencies to put him forward for any suitable position that came up. To do this was firmly in the agency's best interest: Sean had spent over £350,000 in six months and if they could move him to a new position with a big or bigger budget, he'd be taking them with him. As such, "New Job For Sean" became a significant component of their new business strategy. Sean was eventually "headhunted" and left his ailing company a matter of weeks before its collapse to launch a series of digital music channels for a massive media corporation. Two months later, his old advertising agency announced that they had won a major new account to launch a series of digital music channels for a massive media corporation. Sean's campaign was a complete waste of money. Even an A-level business student would have noticed that there was no call to action, but today Sean is quite candid about how he was able to pass the buck:

> The company was desperate, they were just glad that somebody was doing something positive and hearing the brand on the radio and seeing the name in magazines did a lot to raise morale in the short term.
>
> It was easy for me to avoid the question of revenue. I was responsible for raising awareness: which is what I did. Converting that awareness into revenue was someone else's responsibility, although nobody at the company was able to figure out who that someone was. We didn't even have a sales director.

For obvious reasons, Sean and Colm want to remain anonymous, but both of these examples should be considered generic. Simply reading though the pages of the trade and business press, it won't take you long to find many similar examples.

Jeremy Dale was the marketing director at ITV Digital (previously known as ONdigital) where he oversaw the company's famous "Al and Monkey" campaign. ITV Digital was an attempt by Carlton and Granada to wrench the digital TV initiative from Rupert Murdoch's Sky corporation. Not many people have taken on Murdoch and won, or even come out with an honourable draw, and ONdigital's decision to set up in the old offices of the defunct BSkyB – the long forgotten "Squarial" alternative to Sky, crushed by Murdoch less than ten years earlier – looked like it was tempting fate.

The experts all agreed: to succeed, all ITV Digital needed to do was to get absolutely everything right. So when they launched with flaky technology that was supported by a "too good to be true" new subscriber offer (that was indeed too good to be true) and bolstered their content offer with a £300 million spend on the exclusive rights to show second-rate football matches, it's fair to say that the early signs didn't augur well.

Dale's contribution was perceived as a diamond in a coalmine. "Al and Monkey", conceived by creative advertising powerhouse Mother, was undeniably popular and went on to win a host of awards. Monkey's cachet with the British public was such that he outlived his *alma mater*, going on to enjoy a second career as the puppet face of *Children in Need*.

With hindsight, it is difficult to see what message this campaign was actually trying to push to consumers and whether or not it did enough to distinguish the ITV Digital offer from its rival Sky. Whatever Monkey achieved though, it wasn't enough to save ITV Digital from spectacular collapse. In July 2002, with ONdigital dead in the dirt, Orange UK announced it had: "Strengthened its brand marketing team with the appointment of ex-ITV Digital executive Jeremy Dale to the newly-created position of Brand Marketing Director." John Allwood, executive vice-president Orange UK, said: "Jeremy is a skilled and experienced marketer with a proven history of developing compelling brand campaigns – his appointment further strengthens our brand communications team. I am pleased to welcome Jeremy to Orange."

I'm sure Dale is a supremely capable marketer, and I have no evidence that he's ever slacked a day in his life, but I do find it interesting that even in a disaster like ITV Digital, senior executives are still perceived to have played highly successful roles. What could have been a black hole shines out of his CV like a beacon. Like Sean, he knew when to take a risk and by luck or design, managed to engineer an escape route.

Sean and Colm are very different people. Sean is a career marketer while Colm is the living, breathing epitome of the Peter Principle*, for whom slacking is an inevitable side-effect of not actually being equipped to do the job. But, like Sean, there is nothing unique about Colm's position. Many senior executives are winging it and if they do get found out sooner or later – who cares? After a few years in the job, any exit is going to be softened with stacks of cash and share options. In fact, the longer you can hang on in there, the bigger the reward for failure will become.

In November 2004 Sainsbury's announced the first losses in the company's history. This was the final chapter

---

*The "Peter Principle" was first introduced by L. Peter in a humorous book of the same name, describing the pitfalls of bureaucratic organization. The principle, which states that "In a hierarchical structure, people tend to be promoted up to their 'level of incompetence'", is based on the observation that in large organizations, employees typically start in the lower ranks, but when they prove competent at a task they get promoted. The process of climbing up the career ladder continues until the employee reaches a position in which they are no longer competent. At this moment the process usually stops and, since the established rules make it difficult to demote anyone, the net result is that organizations tend to be filled with incompetent people.

in a story of mismanagement that had been emerging since it announced flat sales figures for 2003 (in the wake of 10.2% increases reported by rivals Asda). The board of directors sat and watched as more and more investment was ploughed into the business, in the face of widening gaps in the chairman's strategy. New IT systems failed to work, poor distribution was leaving gaps on the shelves and the stores themselves were starting to look rather tawdry. A fundamental issue: the inability to keep the shelves properly stocked was ignored. Either the board was unaware of what was happening, or more likely it was structured in such a way that responsibility could be shirked and buck-passing was tolerated. Sir John Sainsbury, the company founder, had been so dominant that a "yes men" culture had developed; when he stood down there was no one to give the team the direction that they needed. Executives were not used to challenging the highest authority in the company and they were left so rudderless that trouble was inevitable.

The penalty for this kind of failure is typically an enormous pay-off. As we have seen, Chairman Peter Davies was fired with only a £3.8 million pay-off. He must have been devastated! The company was unequivocal about Sir Peter's performance and the reasons for his departure, accusing him of: "Failing to deliver where it counts." Investors were furious, calling for the cancellation of "bonuses paid for failure" and demanding that the company make a commitment to the novel idea that, in future, bonuses would only be payable for success. Sir Peter's response was: "I am retiring and want to enjoy life out of the public eye."* Which shouldn't be too difficult with £3.8 million in the bank.

In business today, all success is relative and failure is tolerated and rewarded. The lack of clear accountability, shared responsibility and the emergence of woolly jobs and roles make it difficult for businesses themselves to identify internally who is performing and who isn't. For those outside of the company, it is almost impossible. When recruiting staff, companies must rely on value judgements about a candidate's ability based on the performance of their present employer as a whole.

Self-aware City Slackers like Colm can easily exploit the Peter Principle. They understand that by creating greater visibility for themselves externally, they can become easily synonymous with the company's success and distance themselves from inevitable failures, which will increase their attractiveness to potential employers. And the further they climb up the corporate ladder, the bigger the bed of cash waiting to cushion their inevitable fall.

---

*Source: the *Sunday Times*, 21.11.04 ("What a difference a boss makes to ailing retailers").

5 | **Selling England by the Euro**

As we've seen, City Slackers put most of their effort into perception, looking like they're doing a great job. They are unconcerned with winning the war, it's the battle they're interested in. Most products fail, so if you can accept the fact that you're going to be working with failures most of the time, the objective becomes simple: make sure it looks like it's got nothing to do with you. Your hands were tied; the product was poor, sales didn't get enough on the shelves, marketing didn't do enough to push it to customers, PR handled the campaign badly, reviews were poor, product management research was flawed. In light of this, how could anyone expect your aspect of the project to succeed? You did a great job of your aspect of the project in very difficult circumstances – what more could anyone ask?

The irony is that although all businesses rely on sales, in most of them nobody has the responsibility for making sure that the products actually sell. In big companies, different camps have different battles to fight. The sales team doesn't really care how the product sells through – that is how many customers buy it; it needs to win the battle with retail to get the product onto shelves. Its concerns lie with how many they can sell in – that is, how many they can get retailers to order – not how many sell through. It is unusual to meet a sales director who doesn't hate the marketing department with a passion, because they perceive it to be wasting company money that they've worked hard to bring in: "Packaging? Who needs packaging! You give it to me in a brown paper bag and I'll sell it." The sad thing is, more often than not they've got a point.

Whatever "Team Marketing" tells you, it is not interested in sales at all. Only two objectives drive marketers: increasing their status and holding onto their jobs. The insecurity of marketers can be seen in the way that many cling to their advertising agency like a security blanket. The agency, with its network of contacts, presents an obvious escape route should things get tough; a source of new employment opportunities. The relationship is symbiotic. The agency views the marketer as an invoice so, if they're out of work or likely to be, it will serve the agency well if they can get them another job because they'll take the agency with them. This explains why agencies and marketers tend to follow each other around. It also explains why so many marketers will settle for second-rate creative and anodyne campaigns. They're usually happy so long as they've got bigger budgets to spend. The only certainty about agency life is that one day they will lose the account, which is why your agency isn't driven by your sales at all. Its battle is to keep you, the client, happy. This often has as much to do with an annual trip to Wentworth, regular Champions League football tickets and providing a shoulder to cry on as it does the quality of its work and the impact that this has on the sell-through figures.

In addition, the PR department is unlikely to be worrying about how well the products perform. It is busy fighting to make sure that everyone takes notice of its brilliantly executed awareness campaign and the column inches of media coverage that it has generated. In fact, the only people who really care about how the product sells is the accounts department, and they have no power to influence sales at all. As a result, none of the other departments really take much notice of what the bean-counters think until it's too late. So, neither will we.

This lack of synergy allows the City Slacker to focus on their performance – that's "performance" in the artistic, dramatic sense, rather than the practical, results-focused, accountable sense. The City Slacker will put a great deal of effort into the visible elements of their role – meetings and presentations, for example – but will commit the bare minimum of endeavour to everything else. It is far easier to paint a mental picture of serious world-class performance than it is to actually achieve it and as such, City Slackers are naturally attracted to jobs that require them to spend a significant proportion of their time off-site or out of the office. Meetings are food and drink to City Slackers, as fundamental to their trade as mortar to a bricklayer or pipes to a plumber because, as any City Slacker will tell you, an empty desk is a busy desk.

I repeat, City Slackers are not losers. In modern business they are the real winners, reaping rewards without any of the real stresses of modern life. Don't mistake them for the stereotype incompetents, the idlers who are the butt of office jokes, who arrive late, leave early and are commonly regarded as a waste of space. The City Slacker is more likely to be one of the intelligent and respected members of the workforce. They will appear to be among the most productive members of staff, always at the heart of any business success and noticeably uninvolved in any failure. The distinction is that the City Slacker puts all their effort into *looking* like they are doing the job. They are certainly not skivers or malingerers in the traditional sense.

Some years ago Glynn Harrison was working in the PR department of a successful company. To cope with growing sales, the company appointed a new key accounts manager. His name was Toby Rignall and the distinction between slackers and skivers can be seen clearly in his story.

Toby was a good-natured, amiable chap. Heavily built and in his mid-30s with an endearing lack of self-awareness, Toby would talk to anyone, just as long as it was about one of the two things he was interested in: the complete history of British indie music or corny gags. "Happy-go-lucky" is not a term usually associated with salesmen; "terrier-like" or "tenacious" yes, but not "lackadaisical". So it's fair to say that the first impressions of Toby were that he was something of a surprise appointment.

Toby was delighted to have become a company man after more than a decade at the coalface in field and telesales. At the time, Glynn was responsible for the company's public relations* and his only working contact with Toby was in

---

*It might be worth pointing out that Glynn was indeed only concerned with the number of column inches that he could generate for each of his products. Recently, he had been put on a bonus scheme that was linked to sales, until he had argued successfully that the number of units the company sold was down to the sales team and, therefore, something over which he had no control. The company agreed that his bonus would be linked to the amount of coverage that he was able to secure, regardless of its impact on sales. The moral of this story is: there may be no "I" in "team" – but then there isn't a "t", "e", "a" or "m" in "bonus".

the weekly sales and marketing meeting, but they hit it off quite well. Toby discovered that Glynn was into music and began emailing him constantly with questions testing his knowledge of indie ephemera. On the rare occasions that Toby was in the office, he was happy to wander over and spend half an hour discussing this week's new releases, or gigs that he'd caught the previous week. Outside the weekly meeting, they didn't talk about work once.

Toby's job description was surely written in slacker heaven. It was his responsibility to drive round the country in his company car – a brand new, shiny Alfa Romeo – visiting independent retailers under the auspices of ensuring that they were fully stocked up with product, point of sale and sundry marketing materials. His only other responsibility was to ensure that these shopkeepers were fully up to speed with the release schedule and as such, that they were ordering enough stock.

There was a fly in the ointment – Toby's boss, UK sales manager Ian Cosgrove. Bill Hicks, the late American comedian, described bosses "like gnats at a picnic" and if Toby's job was, in fact, a picnic, then Ian was more like a swarm of hornets. Ian had been the previous incumbent in the key accounts role, but was now revelling in his new position. He was experienced enough to know all the tricks and was watching Toby like a sniper. Had Toby been a bona fide City Slacker, Ian's vigilance would have proved no more than an interesting challenge, but unfortunately Toby lacked the wit to slack and simply skived instead.

Toby's performance in the job – even from Glynn's detached position – was toe-curling. It was as if Toby's primary objective was to get fired as quickly as possible: he made every mistake imaginable. Office hours were nominally 9am to 5.30pm. Ian was notoriously the first one in and the last one out. Glynn was not convinced that Ian actually spent all this time working, but it was clearly something he was very proud of, a fact he would wheel out whenever he was embroiled in an argument to highlight his dedication to the company. Toby was required to be in the office only on Mondays to attend the weekly sales and marketing meeting. Initially he treated this as an opportunity to "dress down", arriving in jeans and T-shirt until, in week three, Ian asked him if he'd been decorating. In week four he arrived appropriately suited and booted. Toby invariably rolled in on the dot at 9.35am (blaming traffic). He would disappear for the day at 4.15pm (in order to beat the traffic), which was OK because, as he explained to Ian in a very loud voice, "I've got nothing else to do really." Off he would go, armed with the new CD he'd bought at lunchtime to entertain him on the journey home.

Toby was required to spend Monday making his weekly appointments, which would be submitted to Ian, allowing him to get the heads-up on Toby's activities for that week in advance. Toby's lack of creativity in putting these sheets together was the stuff of legend. He would always start the week (on Tuesday, remember) with an 11am meeting some eight to ten miles away from his home. Friday rarely found him working later than 2.30pm as he typically wound down with a 2pm meeting the same distance away. In-between, his overnight stays on Tuesday, Wednesday and

Thursday had less to do with delivering the company's sales strategy than strategically delivering Toby to that week's biggest gigs, which he'd tell everyone all about the following Monday. Ian would shout over to the PR department: "Glynn, do you know who's playing in Cardiff tonight?" Glynn would respond, after flicking through the NME gig guide, with the name of the appropriate group. At which point Ian would nod knowingly and, addressing the office at large, would shout back: "That explains why Toby's got a meeting there tomorrow morning then."

Toby also appeared unaware that Ian was able to track his progress round the country by simply checking his expenses receipts before signing them off. Toby put absolutely everything through on his company credit card, from scotch eggs and Ginsters pasties to rather dubious claims for "retailer incentives" from HMV and Virgin. He admitted to Glynn that he was completely baffled by how much Ian knew about his whereabouts, and wondered, only half-joking, if he was being followed. On one famous occasion, Toby made an especially foolhardy claim for a movie he'd watched in his hotel room (no gig in town that night – must have been a miscalculation). Unlike his resulting nickname, Toby's claim that, after a hard day out in the field he'd simply kicked back to enjoy *Forrest Gump*, did not gain widespread acceptance, especially as he was unable to give Ian a satisfactory synopsis of the plot. From this point forward everyone in the company knew him as *Forrest Hump*. Another time, Toby admitted to the office at large that he was able to secure free access to every venue in the UK because he was sending the promoters free samples of the company's product in return for free passes.

The final nail in Toby's coffin was in fact a double hammer blow: either would have been sufficient to grant him his marching orders, but both seemed to arrive arm-in-arm. First of all, at the weekly sales and marketing meeting, Toby reported that he'd secured sales orders for the company's next big release of 200 units – out of a total day one ship-out of 20,000.

"It begs the question: why bother?" said the managing director, throwing her pen to the table and folding her arms. Misreading her body language, Toby just laughed: "Don't say things like that, you'll make me start worrying about my job!"

You could have heard a pin drop.

With his future in the balance, you might have expected Toby to rally. Instead, staying true to his rock roots, he saved his best until last and continued to skive with what can only be described as gay abandon.

The second blow came when Sara Elliot, one of the product managers from the marketing department, shadowed Toby for a couple of days to get a better understanding of the independent retail landscape. This had long been planned: Ian was keen for a clandestine report regarding what Toby was actually getting up to while he was out of the office. With the entire company looking at him through the eyes of Sara, Toby made only six appointments. On the first day he picked her up at 10am and made a brief call at 11am to see "an old mate", who failed to make an order. From here it was straight over the road to an Audi dealership. Sara spent an hour on her own in the car while Toby road-tested an Audi A4. One more store visit and they were finished for the day. After checking into the hotel at 4pm, Toby announced that he was going for "my nap" (evidently a daily occurrence) and asked Sara if she fancied going with him to see The Fall in concert later on that evening. The following day, they checked out at 10.30am and made two brief calls to see retailers before Toby took a 40-mile detour to pick up some shelves from his brother-in-law. They were an hour late for the final appointment, by which time the bloke that they were supposed to meet had left for the day. So at 3.30pm, Toby dropped Sara off at the station and drove the remaining eight miles to his home. Presumably he had some DIY to be getting on with.

Toby's "resignation" on the following Monday came as a great surprise to him. It's worth repeating – Toby was no City Slacker, he was just not very good. A City Slacker would never have lost a job in this way. City Slackers are black belts in the art of corporate politics. They do all the things that the business books tell you to do, except they always put themselves before the company. Toby could easily have enjoyed exactly the same lifestyle, if only he had been willing to put a bit of effort into his artistic performance. If we run through Toby's story again with a City Slacker's mind, and think about how we can make things *look* good, it's really not difficult to see where Toby went wrong.

Toby should have understood that his only day in the office was the most important day of the week. It was the only day that his boss had any visibility of his performance. What Ian saw there would colour his view of what he believed was going on when Toby was out of the office. The first thing Toby should have done was to make sure he either arrived for work really early, or really, really late. Getting in early is fine: you don't have to do anything while you're there because there's no one to see you doing it, and rather than make a big deal out of it you can simply say that it's a tactic to beat the traffic.

The *really* smart thing to do, but admittedly more difficult to pull off, is to get in really late. Arriving at 9.35am and blaming the traffic won't get you anywhere, but getting in at 10.35am and blaming the traffic because you've already had an 8-o'clock meeting (or pretended to) with someone you've been "trying to get in with for ages" will be perfectly acceptable.

Having nothing to do is, of course, always great news, but letting your boss know this is obviously a bad idea. Toby should have carved himself out a soft project (with nebulous objectives) that could have easily kept him occupied for months. Perhaps a piece of perceptions research into the retail landscape, or the relative effectiveness of merchandise over PoS would prove useful. This would be interesting for his colleagues and the findings would be difficult to challenge, even if there's no actual value in either study. He could have looked at improving operational efficiency by overhauling the company database (they always need overhauling) or by arranging internal communications meetings so that the other parts of the company can better understand the sales process. These are just a few ideas, but they could have kept him going literally for years.

Toby also had to submit a weekly list of appointments and ring in with regular progress reports. There's no way around this, but again it's an opportunity to shine rather than shirk. If he'd just followed a few simple rules from the City Slacker handbook, the perception of his performance would have been completely different. The more appointments Toby makes, the better. Two things he could have done: first, submit his appointments on a monthly basis (the numbers look bigger); second, he should have upped the number of appointments by 20%. Of course, these would be fictional appointments, half of whom would "cancel" and half of whom wouldn't be actual meetings but telephone conversations. By rotating the cancellations and telephone calls across his range of contacts, after as little as three months the meetings and calls will have blurred to an extent that checking up on him would be impossible. Toby has just made himself 20% more productive.

If you're out of the office, no one really knows where you are – it's best to keep it that way. Ian was able to track Toby's progress across the country because of his expenses and petrol receipts. If you have a company car, only buy petrol in your own town on a Saturday or Sunday. During the rest of the week, never fill up within a 100-mile radius of home. It can be worth driving out of your way to pick up lunch. A receipt from a pub in Gloucester means that you had meetings in Gloucester and a working lunch with a client. A receipt for a brunch bar and can of Diet Coke from an M5 service station means you were bombing up the motorway, probably in order to arrive home early. If you're on the train it's even easier. Just buy train tickets – nobody says you've got to use them. What can't speak can't lie, so if the receipt says you were in Aberdeen on Tuesday, you were in Aberdeen on Tuesday.

Never talk about what you do in the evenings when you're working away. Explain that you arrived after nine and spent a miserable evening working in the hotel room with a room service meal. If you do go out, remember to make it clear that you spent a tiresome evening entertaining clients. Another nice touch is to write your emails at the usual time, but don't send them. When you get back in from the pub, turn on the computer, press "Send" and then turn it off again (an email sent late at night always makes a great impression). If you are at home for the evening, make sure you have your dinner and put the kids to bed before turning the computer on and pressing "Send".

Phoning in reports is another opportunity to underline your dedication. If you're on the train, always make the call when you're between stations: this way you can be sure that no one is going to overhear any announcements that will give away your true location. This means that you can report your location based on what looks best for you, not where you actually are. If it's before 5.30pm, always claim you've only just boarded and are "stuck the other side of Luton". If you're in the car, always maintain that you're further away from home than you really are: "I'm stuck in a car park on the M1 just north of York – I'll be lucky to be home by tomorrow at this rate." Never call the office before 5.30pm to check messages. You can even do this from home, under the pretence of having pulled over at the services for a coffee and to check through some paperwork. Alternatively, sit in the car on the drive with the engine running and pretend to be stuck in a traffic jam.

When reporting activity back to your line manager, always follow the "90% rule". That is to say, always keep back an important piece of news for an emergency – such as an alibi for a fictional meeting if you're running late, for example, or are challenged about what you've been doing. And always be sure to make it clear that you've only just found out about this (after all, you wouldn't want anyone to think you're keeping stuff back from them). In your activity report, always include soft projects and always talk about things in development as well as things you have done. This is a really simple way of making you sound twice as busy and, as it's arguably relevant, nobody will think it unusual. Also, at the end of your weekly report, always invite colleagues to give you comment and feedback outside the meeting. Not only are you unlikely to get this, but it will make you sound confident and conscientious.

This is basic ABC stuff for the City Slacker, but it takes slightly more experience to combat the double jeopardy that eventually did for Toby. The logic was: it is Toby's responsibility to deliver sales, he has only delivered 200 – therefore, he should be fired. Toby made it too simple for them; even though it's unlikely that the best salesman in the world could have done much better. In this case, attack was Toby's best source of defence. In impersonal, indirect terms, he should have stated that he was furious with the figures. Then he should have explained that, naturally, his first reaction was that the retailers had let them down, but rather than throw his rattle out of the pram, he had decided to dig deeper. At this point he could pull in as many reasons as he likes: the retailers thought it was the wrong kind of product, his retailers felt that they were poorly supported, competitor sabotage, macro issues affecting the market, ineffective marketing (which obviously his soft project is designed to address), distribution problems, disappointing PR, poorly researched development, etc. The point is, as we've seen, accountability and responsibility are so disparate that it is easy for everyone to own a success. City Slackers realize that the same principles can be applied to failure. There will be some truth in every reason Toby gives. Remember, his objective is not to ensure that the problem gets solved, but simply to keep his job.

Finally, had he but known it, Toby's shadow – Sara from product marketing – provided him with the best opportunity of all. As any marketer will tell you, the best endorsement of all is a third-party testimonial. *We* can tell you how good our thing is as much as we like, but deep down you know we're trying to sell it to you. If, however, *they* tell you how good it is, when clearly there is no benefit to them for doing so, why wouldn't you believe them? Indeed, impartial testimonial is a powerful weapon in the marketing arsenal.

Toby should have used this opportunity to demonstrate how hard he was working. He should have picked Sara up at half-five in the morning and crammed a week's worth of meetings into two days. He could still have seen his mates, but rather than patting them on the back, asking them to put the kettle on and chatting about football for 20 minutes, he could have engineered a couple of "difficult meetings". One could have threatened to send all the stock back, only to be talked out of it by Toby ("All right – but only because it's you!"). Another could have been unwilling to take any stock at all until Toby presented him with a couple of "incentives" from HMV, while a third could have been briefed to have been as relentlessly rude as possible.

At the end of day one, Toby should have made sure that he put in a three-hour drive, using the excuse that the first appointment the next day was typically "impossible to get in to see", and gallantly dropped an exhausted Sara off at her house in the early hours of the morning. By the time he was back in the office, the news would have spread about what an awful job Toby had and how hard he was working with unreasonable people in difficult circumstances.

The modern business environment provides City Slackers with ample opportunities to work creatively. This illusion of industry is endemic and I suspect that there are many organizations in which City Slackers outnumber those whose efforts are genuinely driving the business forward. Recently I was asked to audit the structure of the marketing department of a large media company. The senior manager's perception of the performance they were getting out of their marketing manager was in stark contrast to that held by her peers and support staff. While office politics could certainly have played a part in this I found it telling that, when pressed, two of her senior managers were unable to explain what her objectives were and were also at a loss to explain how her performance was measured. Reading through a copy of her job description didn't provide them with any answers either.

There is a truism that states that no employee is indispensable or irreplaceable. This doesn't go far enough: as I have said, many companies could dispense with many members of staff without making any replacements and would not notice any dip in productivity.

If we return to the example of Toby, the company in question simply didn't need a key accounts manager. The products still would have found their way onto the shelves; there would have been no loss of efficiency. This is not at all unusual because as organizations grow, new positions evolve from functions already being carried out by existing members of the workforce.

Small organizations may begin with only a commercial director, but given the right conditions this genus will spawn, in turn, new and distinct species. No sooner have they begat a sales manager and a marketing manager, then these new entities will also spawn: product managers, key accounts managers, trade marketing executives, PR managers and so on, in a glorious parallel to Darwin's theory of evolution.

The underlying principle of evolution, "the survival of the fittest", is often misunderstood. In the Victorian sense, "fittest" simply means the "most appropriate", not "best" or "strongest". This explains why, in the face of the urbanization of the planet during the last 200 years, strong tigers have been driven to the brink of extinction while, despite the best efforts of pest controllers, relatively weedy rats outnumber humans in most of our cities and towns.

The City Slacker has evolved to exploit the opportunity presented by modern corporate structures. They understand that careers in commerce are a struggle for survival and that, ironically, they will earn the best living from roles which, sensibly, could be made redundant. These are the environmental conditions that allow them to devote their time instead to creating a mirage of productivity.

6 | "Our Survey Says ..." News Out of Nothing

Of all the fields covered in this book – the worlds of marketing, sales, advertising, technology and the media – there is arguably none more maligned than the field of public relations.

In 2004 there were an estimated 35,000 people working in PR in the UK. This is a relatively small number of employees and the popularity of the sector means that competition for jobs – especially at graduate level – is very tough indeed*.

The Chartered Institute of Public Relations (CIPR) describes the UK PR sector as "the most highly developed in Europe". A combination of private and public organizations spent almost £2.5 billion on PR services in 2003. According to CIPR, the industry is growing at a rate of approximately 17% per year and all of the FTSE 100 companies have public relations departments.

You might expect PR to attract more than its fair share of City Slackers, but in fairness there is much more to the discipline than meets the eye and it is just as well represented with industrious, capable individuals as any other profession. The interesting thing is that the nature of the work undertaken by PRs provides City Slackers with a number of unique opportunities that aren't to be found in marketing, advertising sales or the media.

---

*Source: 2004 Survey by Prospects.ac.uk, the UK's official graduate careers website.

The term "public relations" is something of a misnomer. PRs don't really have any relationship with the public; they affect the relationship between clients and their audiences by managing their profile in the appropriate media. Traditionally, PRs entered the profession from the related fields of marketing or journalism, but an increasing number of new entrants arrive directly from college, usually clutching a degree in media or communications studies, without a background in either.

The responsibility for PR varies from organization to organization. In many, PR sits within the remit of the marketing team, either as an in-house department or as a direct report from an external consultancy, but there are an equal number of instances where PR works very efficiently standing on its own. For example, in public sector and political organizations which have little to market but a duty to communicate, the profile of corporate heads of communications – such as New Labour's former head of spin, Alastair Campbell, or the FA's David Davies – can be considerable.

The Chartered Institute of Public Relations defines PR as: "The planned and sustained effort to establish and maintain goodwill and mutual understanding between an organization and its publics." This is a broad definition and rightly so, because the manner in which PR is implemented is almost as various as the organizations themselves. Used well, PR is without doubt the most effective and powerful means of pushing a message and influencing popular opinion. In those PR-led organizations it is usually a strategic discipline in its own right, critical to the success of the business itself. Think of Virgin, for whom no new product launch would be complete without Richard Branson abseiling in on a camel dressed as Widow Twanky with a pretty girl on either arm. In contrast, many companies view it as no more than a cheap (if largely inefficient) substitute for marketing. Here, PR is used as an add-on to drive either sales leads or sales themselves, with little thought to what actually can be achieved and so, understandably, the results are usually disappointing.

The sector of PR that we are interested in is the realm of consumer PR. Of the £2.5 billion spent on PR in the UK in 2003, the bulk – around 76% – was spent trying to push a message directly to consumers. Consumer PR can be defined as that employed by companies with products or services to sell. They use PR specialists to get the media to write about these products and services so that people will buy them. With all that money floating about, it is not surprising that it is a highly competitive and difficult sector of the market.

The problems involved in delivering a successful PR campaign are complex, but I'll attempt to summarize them. First, PRs don't control or own the media so they're not in a position to guarantee coverage, not even to themselves, which makes results and outcomes difficult to predict. Knowing how well or badly a campaign will go comes only through assimilation and experience; it's not something that can really be taught, despite the best attempts of universities and training companies. Furthermore, because PRs are relying on third parties – usually journalists – to deliver the results, they are never really in control. Experienced PRs know that it's never in print until it's in print. Stories fail to appear for many different reasons, none of which are the PRs fault. They are "moved", "pulled", "shelved" or "spiked" all the time, depending upon how much "news" there is available to fill the pages. Whatever the reason – a natural disaster or a celebrity indiscretion – PRs are no better than anyone else at predicting the future, so if they happen to tell the client that their story is in the paper next Friday, then they should know that they run the risk of receiving a disappointed phone call demanding to know why it isn't.

Second, there is the practical question of making the story interesting. The press wants people stories, the consumer PRs have got product stories, so to get the necessary amount of coverage the campaign must contain an element of human interest. This can be done in a number of ways: wacky pictures, celebrity endorsements, media stunts or commissioning a survey, for example. But whatever the tactics, it inevitably results in a protracted process of barter during which the PR negotiates a level of product coverage in return for providing human interest material. Wherever possible, they try to play competing magazines or papers off against each other in an attempt to secure the maximum amount of column inches for the client.

The final, and salient, problem for PRs is the clients themselves. Fact: no client's business, product or service is half as interesting as it thinks it is. Let us imagine that you make spoons for a living and that is all you do. It's probably fair to say that, in time, spoons will become quite important to you. You might subscribe to a trade paper called *Spoon Weekly*, you may have a small collection of books on the history of spoon-making lying around the house, you may even record any spoon-related programmes that you come across on TV with a view to forming a definitive library. If there is another company making spoons across the road you will probably loathe them, and in conversation with your partner over dinner you may occasionally mention how much you abhor their shoddy workmanship and poor business practice. Then one day, your company invents a new way of making spoons – the best ever, a groundbreaking design that will change the face of spoon-making forever. At this point you will probably get quite excited and you might well decide to hire a PR agency to promote your new invention to the world, dreaming of interviews on World At One and colour spreads in the *Sunday Times Magazine*. The reality is that the world is going to be far less interested in your invention than you are and the level of coverage that you are going to achieve won't be giving Britney Spears any nightmares. But if you do want to give it a try, there are plenty of PRs out there who would be happy to take your £12,000 a month budget and give it their best shot.

Consumer PR has a lot to make it attractive to City Slackers. For a start, there's a lot of money to be earned from PR and it is widely perceived to be an exciting, glamorous profession. New entrants (or "fresh meat", as they are often referred to) labour under the delusion that they'll be working with big brands, meeting celebrities and will probably get to go to lots of parties. But most important of all for the budding City Slacker is that because of these difficulties, PR is notorious for being the most difficult service to audit or measure.

PRs can't really make any promises. They rely on contacts, reputation, their ability to think creatively and their powers of persuasion to get the job done, but any PR will tell you that the crucial element of the mix is the quality of the story. PRs have a symbiotic relationship with the media based on a mutual antipathy that is tempered by necessity. Usually, the only way that a journalist is going to get the story is by going through the PR, and the only way that the PR is going to please the client is by getting the journalist to run with the story. More often than not, the effectiveness of the campaign is down to what is in the client's head. The industry itself recognizes this and PRs can take several courses that deal simply with "How to Manage Client Expectations". Even the Institute of Public Relations struggles with the concept of accountability. There is no industry standard measurement and the Institute's own recommended PRE (Planning, Research and Evaluation) system is cumbersome, rarely used and difficult to understand for those outside the sector.

Most practitioners rely on simpler mechanics: converting editorial into an advertising-value equivalent, numbers of media hits or opportunities to see; or more often than not, simply not bothering at all on the grounds that if the client is happy, they're happy and if they're not, no amount of pie charts, graphs and analysis is going to convince them otherwise.

While none of this is necessarily a problem, and neither does it invalidate the benefits of a well-executed PR campaign as one of the most effective means of communicating with the market, it does provide plenty of scope for those seeking to avoid being accountable.

The reputation of PRs – as lunching freeloaders who would spin the Final Solution if it paid them a £7,000 a month retainer – is on the whole unfair, but there is undoubtedly a sizeable minority who deserve every stereotype that you can throw at them. And you won't have to look very far to find them either.

Ian Rollins is an independent producer. Ian has been making documentaries for ten years, but much of his bread-and-butter money comes from working on big budget, short films for the blue-chip clients of large advertising agencies. What the work lacks creatively it certainly makes up for financially.

Ian specializes in "The Making of ..." films. When companies like Pepsi or Gap, for example, shoot a TV ad featuring Madonna or Britney Spears, Ian will shadow the director and film interviews with the talent, backroom team and marketing personnel. The results are put together on DVD to form an electronic press kit (EPK), which the PR agency can use to generate editorial coverage in print or through broadcast.

One of Ian's biggest clients is the manufacturer of a well-known snack food. Recently they have undergone a major internal and external restructuring and, as a result, have appointed new advertising, PR and creative agencies. With a new campaign imminent, the marketing director thought it would be a good idea for all his external service providers to get together for a meet-and-greet and to plan the project in detail.

At the meeting there were a lot of new faces around the table, including the new PR team from one of the biggest

PR agencies in Europe. They represented some of the biggest names in entertainment as well as some of the biggest household brands. In order to break the ice with so many strangers, the person leading the meeting thought it would be a good idea to start by asking everyone to introduce themselves and – to make it fun – offer up a piece of personal information in the process. Like a scene from an Alcoholics Anonymous meeting, they went round the table:

"Hi, I'm Rebecca. I'm a production assistant, and I've just got back from a skiing holiday in France."

Everyone smiled and nodded and they moved clockwise round the table.

"My name's Mark. I'm a creative director, but my real passion is kick-boxing and I'm taking part in the UK championships for the first time next weekend."

Everyone smiled and nodded and they moved clockwise round the table.

"Hello everyone, my name is Michelle and I'm an account manager. I like cooking Thai food and am taking an evening class in stand-up comedy."

Everyone smiled, a few even chuckled, and so it went on around the table until they reached Adrian, the account director from the PR agency. Adrian didn't speak. He just stood up, reached into his pocket and threw his car keys down onto the table before sitting down with his arms folded and a rather self-satisfied smirk on his face. There was a brief pause, punctuated by puzzled glances, before he decided the moment was right to break the silence by declaring:

"Yes. It's a Lamborghini!"

To set up a PR consultancy you need two pieces of equipment: a phone and a computer with internet access. A website might be an advantage – just make sure it is filled with glowing testimonials. Obviously you won't have any from clients yet, but quotes from journalists saying how great you are probably will be enough to be going on with. Now all you need to do is find yourself some clients.

PRs are the ultimate middlemen, but like magicians the nuances of their trade are a closely-guarded secret. Many people – including almost all journalists – believe that PRs are little more than glorified couriers delivering news and assets from their clients, who don't tell the truth and will always let spin get in the way of the story. Clients see a very different side. PRs offer them the opportunity to actually control what is written about them, where and when. They have arcane power, the tantalizing ability to control what people think; wouldn't you want to pay to have some of that? You may suspect that many PRs aren't up to much, but then Lamborghinis aren't cheap, which suggests that quite a few other people are very happy to pay a great deal of money for whatever it is they do for them.

The biggest agencies turn over tens of millions in fees alone, with growth coming from the acquisition of new accounts. Like most service businesses that only have time to sell, all the best PR people (and the best paid) will be responsible for generating new business. What this means is that, in order to pay for the Lamborghinis, the most impressive people in the agency will be spending their time selling to clients and not working with the media on their behalf. One rule of thumb: if you are ever getting PR agencies in to pitch, never base your decision on how impressive the person doing the presentation is. Their role is to sell to you, which explains why you're so impressed. Instead, pay particular attention to the junior people sitting next to them, because it is they who will be doing all the important work on your account.

In 1999, Kelvin McPherson was working in-house as a PR executive when he was headhunted by one of the UK's top PR consultancies. They had just won a contract to launch a new video games console and wanted Kelvin to join the team as account manager. Kelvin did a sterling job – earning himself a nomination as PR Executive of the Year in the industry awards – and the client was delighted with the coverage. It was a dream account. The client loved the job that Kelvin and his agency was doing, the impact was highly visible, so there were no sticky arguments over fees and no unnecessary time wasted filling out contact reports.

But all was not what it seemed. There were a couple of things that the client didn't know about the way that their account was being handled. First, Kelvin was working on the account on his own. He wasn't even full-time because in addition he was working on projects for a leading chocolate manufacturer and a Premiership football club. His boss – the account director – attended a monthly client meeting along with Kelvin that was both the beginning and end of his involvement with the account. Second, Kelvin was being paid £28,000 a year. The client was basically paying £300,000 a year in fees for a third of his time. It's possible to see how they could have got better service for half the money.

As I said at the beginning of the chapter, it is the nature of PR work that creates a unique opportunity for City Slackers. The weight of all this £2.5 billion worth of effort comes crashing down on the media. True, newspapers have many pages to fill, but what they want is stories and what they get is press releases. They are literally overpowered by useless press releases that clog up email inboxes and fax machines and, in the majority of cases, are followed up with at least one phone call asking whether they received the release and are they planning to do anything with it? The *Media Guardian* editor routinely receives around 200 requests for features per day. Let us allow him 20 seconds to read and delete each one and then, let's say, only 60% are followed up with a phone call that lasts on average 30 seconds. This conservative estimate means that he will be spending just over two hours every day on this fruitless activity.

Derek Douglas is a sub-editor at a national red-top tabloid where the news team has developed an interesting solution for dealing with this. The paper publishes a newsdesk fax number to which all press releases can be submitted for consideration. The number is linked to a fax machine which, consequently, spews out press releases ceaselessly for ten hours a day. The fax machine feeds directly into a large dustbin. Occasionally, one of the news team will wander across and pick out a release at random. He will then read it out to the amusement and entertainment of the rest of the team.

Getting their clients into the press is no cakewalk, which is why PRs are always keen to stress the value of their contacts and relationships with the press. But this is not necessarily bad news, because the harder it becomes to get their clients in, the more they can charge for their services. A client happy with the level of coverage that they are receiving is one who may well be happy to increase their retainer.

The truth is that a PR is only as good as the story that they are promoting. Natalie Corner is an account manager at a large Manchester consultancy. Two accounts that she is working on concurrently are an international film festival – at which Alan Yentob is the keynote speaker – and the launch of the tenth album from underground chillout act Fila Brasilia. The contrast between the two accounts couldn't be more stark. The job on Alan Yentob involved sifting through a host of interview requests from broadcast, national press, trade and monthly magazines; fielding dozens of calls from editors and journalists with offers of coverage and presenting the client with a recommendation for where the interviews should appear to maximize the impact of the campaign. The Fila Brasilia campaign involved making over 700 phone calls, attending numerous meetings and pulling in a raft of favours to secure just 23 media hits. There is no question which of the two campaigns required more effort but in PR, more than any other discipline, there are no rewards for endeavour.

The drive for new business requires that PR agencies push their credentials; as a result, the quality of their contacts takes centre stage. A peculiar boast, one might think, like measuring your achievement by the success of your friends. But as these testimonials from the homepage of Freud Communications'* website demonstrate, it's not what you know:

> "Number one for PR, Freud Communications – we love it."
> Rebekah Wade, Editor, the *Sun*.

> "Freud Communications is a big friend of the *Sunday Times* Business Section. We trust them and that is what really matters."
> William Lewis, Editor, *Sunday Times Business*.

There's no doubting Freud's credentials – they've earned their blue-chip client list and good luck to them – but the point is, William and Rebekah love Freud because of their client list. How keen they are to run your story, regardless of who's trying to sell it, is really down to how interesting it is on a scale of one to ten (with new spoons scoring a big fat zero and the love life of David Beckham an 11 or 12). No PR enjoys pushing a difficult story. They'd all take a "Yentob" over a "Fila Brasilia" every time and this is what makes the PR City Slacker so interesting, because most of them can be found working on the best accounts. Take the Yentob example. The performance of the best and the worst PRs will look relatively similar. The media wants to interview him, so even the most prosaic of individuals is going to be able to deliver an impressive set of clippings to their client. Not so with the spoons story, where it will take

---

*Freud Communications is one of the most UK's most successful and better-known agencies representing corporate clients like AOL, Nike, Pepsi, swanky London watering hole Soho House and celebrities like Ryan Giggs, Steve Coogan and Chris Evans.

countless negative phone calls, a great deal of pleading, a huge amount of creativity and several quiet news days in a row to get anything at all.

In all the entertainment sectors – films, games, music and TV – the PRs with the worst reputations are invariably those with the biggest titles and ultimately the least work to do. In the late 1990s the UK's video games publishers, oblivious to the savage consolidation that would rip through the industry over the next five years, were in ebullient mood. The Sony PlayStation had arrived and promised to deliver a truly mass market from which all would prosper. As the cash poured in, companies expanded, marketing departments got bigger and advertising campaigns became more ambitious. Head and shoulders above everyone else, then as now, was the American giant Electronic Arts (EA). The first publisher to pursue a market-led rather than a product-led development strategy, EA was also the only company to realize that this move into the mainstream would mean that the games themselves would have to change. It was this vision, as much as the quality of their games, that has seen them achieve global domination of their market.

Against this backdrop, any fool could have run EA's PR department, and if the allegations of UK specialist games press is to be believed, they sometimes did. During this period, the respect for EA's extraordinarily consistent products was inversely proportional to the lack of respect for their PR machine. The press alleged that EA's in-house team was incommunicado, that their calls often went unreturned, that information was difficult to get hold of and that there was little proactive campaigning on behalf of even the pillar titles. Grumbling journalists should never be taken too seriously, and EA's games certainly never seemed to suffer from a lack of coverage from where I, and indeed most of the UK's gamebuying public, was sitting.

But then a very interesting thing happened. One of the incumbent PR team was headhunted by a large pan-European PR agency to head up a new division. The agency in question had been trying to break into the video games market without much success for two years. They had discovered that the industry was a closed shop, served by specialists who had entrenched relationships with the major publishers. Their logic was easy to follow: "What we need to do is bring in a heavyweight from the games industry, then we will be taken seriously. But how do we find the best person for the job? Well, EA is the best company, so it follows that they must have the best PR person." The point is, just because you're working on the best products doesn't mean you're going to be as effective when you are asked to promote something even slightly inferior. The PR manager at Not Very Good Games Limited might actually be a genius, handsomely remunerated for his ability to turn sows ears, if not into silk purses, then at least into serviceable wallets. If the agency wanted to recruit the best, then their strategy was flawed

In order to generate coverage or, more especially as one agency puts it, "to make news out of nothing", PRs are required to think creatively and this usually manifests itself in events or (as they are known colloquially) publicity stunts. Every day, hundreds of PR stunts are taking place round the country. They vary enormously in terms of scale and complexity, due largely to the client's budget: anything from an "exclusive" picture of Nell McAndrew or some other C-list fame junkie dressed as a nurse holding up a new brand of suppository, to a bloke on stilts holding up traffic while distributing a particular brand of meat pie.

What most of these publicity stunts have in common is that they fail to generate any coverage whatsoever. But this doesn't really matter to the City Slacker, because it is much easier to mobilize a bloke on stilts than it is to make 700 phone calls. And if it fails to score a hit with the media, at least the client will be able to see how busy they are. That the stunt is a failure is not really an issue. At worst it can be written off as an awareness exercise and, like a champion angler, PRs are good at "bigging up" the near misses they've had, the ones that got away. Within the client company, the PR agency's PR will be managed by the person responsible for commissioning them to do the job. No marketing director is going to admit to appointing a bunch of yahoos on a £120,000 annual retainer, which makes life easier for everyone.

One other thing to remember is that the publicity stunts you read or hear about are invariably the successful ones and no matter how lame they sound (it's amazing how many celebrities will be willing to change their name by deed poll to promote a can or beer or a bottle of condiment*), they are nothing compared to the ones that

---

*Jimmy Brown né White and Julia Heineken formerly Carling, to name but two.

didn't work, which in every single case seemed like a great idea at the time, were signed off by somebody who should have known better, and were paid for with hard cash. The following are just a few genuine examples of events that you didn't read about. I like to put this into context by thinking of all the time and money spent on these events every day and then brainstorming possible solutions to alleviate world poverty.

First up, a contender for the most badly timed mail-out. In August 2003, the UK was in the midst of the hottest summer since records began. The PRs responsible for the "repositioning of the Stilton Cheesemakers' Association" thought that this would be the perfect moment to send journalists a 4lb block of the product. By post. One journalist was actually sick at her desk. Colleagues couldn't decide which smelled worse. On a cheese-related theme, the makers of Emmenthal awarded a £56,000 contract in 2003 to a PR agency who promised to deliver a "national broadcast, press and consumer magazines to target ABC1 housewives, focusing on why the cheese has its distinctive holes". Bringing new meaning to the concept of "news out of nothing" feature coverage in the national press was surprisingly unforthcoming.

The PR team responsible for a product launch event for a local shopping centre came up with a winning visual: consumers wading into a jacuzzi filled with mashed potatoes in search of hidden money. Unfortunately the day set for the "Extreme Mash for Cash" event coincided with a victory parade for the local football team, who had registered a surprise victory in the FA Cup, which for some reason stole away most of the local media. A lone photographer showed up just in time to catch a rowdy contestant as he swan-dived headfirst into the tub. Seconds later, he came up with a cut on his head that was bleeding profusely. "Before I could yell, 'Stop!' he just dived," explained the account director in a photo story the following day, headlined: "Local Man is Victim of Extreme PR Stunt."

One PR covering the Athens Olympics for his client, a home electronics manufacturer, enraged journalists by emailing them what *Mobile News Magazine* described as "a trivial press release" on the much-hyped Olympic torch relay. The magazine's "White Lines" column said: "Email meltdown was caused by 8Mb of attachments showing a C-list celebrity prancing round London in a tight Samsung T-shirt." World telemedia editor Paul Skeldon ranted: "Please do not send me shite like this again. There should be a law against useless PR people sending out massive emails."

To promote a DVD based on the experiences of SAS veteran Andy McNab, a dozen lifestyle journalists were taken on a day's training at a military assault course. One of the hacks, Danny, a freelancer who earned his living by being paid by the word, dislocated a shoulder when he fell 20 feet from a death slide. Danny later described the fall with typical hyperbole as "the most excruciatingly painful experience of my relatively pain-free existence. I can't believe childbirth comes close." At the time of the accident, with Danny lying on the floor, gasping for breath through a blanket of pain, the company PR responsible for the event, Fergus, responded in an appropriate manner by laughing till he cried. "You looked hilarious," he told a recovering Danny the following week, "just like a dying swan!" Thankfully, the tale is not without a happy ending. Having endured a 25-minute wait for the ambulance to arrive, Danny, now only semi-conscious, was finally stretchered off to hospital. As he was being carried away, Fergus, consummate professional to the last, left him with this immortal parting shot:

"Don't worry, mate – I'll drop a press pack off at your office on my way home."

The PR leading the campaign for a new winter sports video game thought it would be a great idea to take a group of reviewers for a week's skiing in Val D'Isère. When the publisher found out that no fewer than six of his editorial staff were away on a spurious "press trip", he was understandably less than delighted. Upon their return, the hacks were roundly chastized and, in order to deter other games manufacturers who may have ideas about organizing similar junkets, barred them from "filling the mags with PR puff". So, no coverage, but at least some journalists learned to ski.

Finally, I was part of a large team responsible for the launch of a new internet technology from BT. Like many large organizations, BT had a list of preferred third-party suppliers, which meant I was unable to use my own PR agency for the launch. The account manager from the preferred supplier attended a meeting to explain his idea for the launch event. It was simplicity itself. We were going to hire a train, drive it round the country picking up journalists along the way, who would then be entertained with "pizzas and quizzes". Once we were full, it was full steam ahead to BT headquarters in Hemel Hempstead, where the delighted hacks would get the opportunity to actually *see the technology itself* (which, in truth, consisted of no more than a roomful of servers). Horrified looks were exchanged. We said we'd get back to them – and did, by duly firing them.

Let's be honest: is all this nonsense really down to City Slackers? For PRs, putting the ball in the client's court is the kiss of death, because the client inevitably ends up taking their ball home with them. This is why PRs need to be proactive, they need to come up with ideas to keep the client happy. If some fool's got £56,000 to spend promoting the holes in their cheese, then it's probably not the right time to have a crisis of conscience, but it probably *is* the right time to come up with some stunt that just might work*.

A sum like £2.5 billion equals a lot of companies and products being promoted. Not everyone in PR is spinning the Iraq War or trying to keep Robbie Williams in the papers. Just about everything – even holes in cheese – is "PR-able". The very best campaigns – for our purposes, let's say those that win awards – are testament to this. The following is a list of some of the winning consumer campaigns from the Institute of Public Relations PRide Awards 2004:

- National Insect Week (Royal Entomological Society)
- Why Spend Spring Cleaning? (Vileda)

---

*It's worth remembering – this was the winning pitch. There were two other agencies presenting whose ideas didn't pass muster.

- Giant Quality Street Tin (Nestlé Quality Street)
- Fox's Cubs Storytelling (Fox's Confectionery)
- NPower Customer Contact Centres (NPower)
- Scoring with Footie Chick (Footie Chick)
- National Game Playing Week (Hasbro)
- "Beauty of Wales" Stamps (Royal Mail Group)
- Get Onboard with Traditional Play! (Zapf Creation)
- Hungry Horse Karaoke Krazy (Hungry Horse)

I'm not decrying the value of these campaigns, I'm sure the clients were delighted with the coverage, and clearly there's a great deal of creativity involved in making these stories newsworthy. But let's just be clear: this list represents the very best.

At the start of this chapter, I said that public relations is one of the most maligned of professions and that PRs are maligned most of all by journalists. By and large, journalists view the relationship as parasitic, not symbiotic, and I hope that more than a few of them would be entertained by this exposition of the discipline. Less so, however, the next chapter, where we turn our attention to the City Slackers who earn their living from within the nation's print and broadcast media.

7 | **Where the Reader Comes First**

In December 2004, Prince Charles – that insightful social commentator – found himself widely derided in the media for some typically ill-considered comments made about one of the big issues of the day. In a leaked memo, providently timed to appear just before the final of *Pop Idol*, the prince brought his considerable, real-world experience to bear on the subject of youthful ambition:

> [People think they can be] pop stars, High Court judges, brilliant TV presenters or infinitely more competent heads of state without ever putting in the necessary work or having the natural ability.

Architects specializing in anything other than mock-Georgian will have breathed a sigh of relief. There's certainly nothing unusual about the prince putting his foot in it, nor indeed about his jaw-dropping lack of self-awareness. But rather than simply logging this as yet another reason to support republicanism and wishing that the Prince of Wales would dedicate his own time to something more constructive – like writing a sequel to *The Old Man of Lochnagar* – it's worth considering that there might be a kernel of truth in what he's saying. Unlike Charles, I don't believe people think that they *can* all be pop stars or even High Court judges, but I do think it's true to say that they *want* to be. There's an old saying, patently untrue but oft-quoted by smart alecs who didn't do very well at school: "Those that can, do. Those that can't, teach." I'd like to appropriate this phrase with an addendum: "Those that can, do. Those that can't teach, write about it."

The technological revolution of the 1980s had an unbelievable impact on the publishing industry. Prior to the invention of desktop publishing (DTP), pioneered by Apple on their Macintosh computer, publishing magazines was an expensive and time-consuming enterprise. As a student in the mid-1980s, I spent far too much time editing the university newspaper. The job involved typing up handwritten copy on a mechanical typewriter, laying out the text on big layout grids with sticky tape and copious notes to the printer written in an arcane language. We did have an electric typewriter, which possessed the amazing function of being able to erase the previous five letters, but that was the preserve of the few members of staff who could touch type. Mistakes were inevitable and frequently hilarious, because the first time we got to see the pages was when the paper hit the news-stands. On one occasion we led with a powerful image of industrial conflict that showed police and striking miners engaged in armed combat. A powerful story requires a powerful headline, and ours read: "Protest Ends with More Police Brutality." The power of the headline was largely diminished by the accompanying image, which showed two men enjoying a thermos of tea and a sandwich, resulting from the fact that printers had misunderstood the arcane script and published the wrong half of the photograph.

The emergence of DTP took much of the power away from printers and made the creation of professional-looking magazines a relatively cheap exercise. As a direct consequence, the sector enjoyed a huge boom during the 1990s. In 1989 there were 4,185 trade and business publications and 2,199 consumer magazines published in the UK; by the end of the following decade these figures had increased to 5,713 and 3,174 respectively. Today an estimated 80% of all adults – and 84% of women – regularly buy a magazine, with almost 3,500 consumer titles from which to choose. Entire publishing organizations have been built on the back of the DTP boom. One of the UK's biggest specialist magazine publishers for example, Future Networks, began life in 1986 with a £1,000 loan and one title: *Your Sinclair*. Today, this unique success of Thatcher's Enterprise Allowance Scheme sells over 1.5 million magazines each month in the UK alone and employs over 1,000 people. In 2004, it made more than £20 million profit.

This massive growth in output is mirrored in all areas of the media. The digital boom in TV and radio production – from four channels to more than 400 – coupled with the need for online content to populate countless websites, means that there has never been an easier time to earn a living as a writer. Demand for the written word is huge.

Traditionally, journalism has never been considered a graduate career. Entrants for the professional qualification, the NCTJ, are not required to have a degree. Cub reporters left school at 16 – at best equipped with just a clutch of O-levels – and learned their trade on local papers. The very talented worked their way up through the regional dailies and onto the newsdesks of the nationals or even the BBC.

Broadcast journalists followed a similar career path through local radio or television. On the whole, jobs were scarce and poorly paid. The media explosion has resulted in many more pages to fill and, by happy coincidence, the nation's universities are now filled with media studies, communications studies and journalism graduates who are only too eager to fill them.

The bright young things emerging from academia, proudly clutching a 2:1 and copy of their dissertation on "The Sociological Influence of Reality TV", don't necessarily want to become film-makers, pop stars, musicians, footballers, racing drivers, novelists, games designers or even High Court judges, but they are savvy enough to know that the trappings of these glamorous professions can be enjoyed by the altogether more achievable route of getting a job to write about them as a lifestyle journalist.

The first reality check comes when they actually start to look for work. Ask a graduate who wants to become a magazine writer what it is they want to write about. Nine times out of ten they'll reply that ideally they'd like to do something in the entertainment or sports fields. Despite the huge increase in media jobs, there is still a huge oversupply of people wanting to do them. A weekly scan of the jobs section in the *Media Guardian* will reveal a dearth of "*Total Film* requires staff writer – no experience necessary" positions, but plenty of the "Wanted: Deputy Editor for *Caged and Aviary Bird Fancier*. Five years' experience minimum" variety. The reason is simple: the popular publications are inundated with speculative applications so they don't need to advertise for staff. Stick an advert in the *Media Guardian* for "Sports Writer – no experience necessary" and you'll be able to take your pick from around 500 applications.

Like all the other so-called creative sectors where there are few clear entry points, lifestyle journalism is no exception. While students tend to see a first or even a second-class media studies qualification as the passport to an exciting career, many editors still only consider those who have had some practical experience. The competition for the limited places on in-house training schemes at magazines and newspapers, or even for work experience, is contested fiercely, with the prize usually consisting of the opportunity to live in very expensive central London and work at least ten hours a day for absolutely nothing. In one not untypical instance, I once received an application from someone who had spent over 12 months working for free on a lifestyle magazine. He had his own desk, computer and security pass – everything, in fact, apart from the salary. Still, for the lucky few who have beaten off the competition successfully or pulled in familial favours (nepotism is rife in publishing), there's the opportunity to land a job with a four-figure starting salary, which consists of little more than airing your opinion for public consumption. They may well have about as much knowledge or feel for their chosen subject as Prince Charles does for social commentary, but given the difficulties they've endured to land their poorly-paid position, it's not surprising that they will be very pleased with themselves.

Polly Hudson is now a showbiz/lifestyle writer at the *Daily Mirror*, but a few years ago she was cutting her journalistic teeth on the celebrity photomontage that is *heat* magazine. You've probably never heard of her, but you'll be familiar with her celebrity lifestyle – it's the same as the ones she writes about. Polly goes to great lengths to point out just how much better her life is than yours in this candid interview with the *Guardian*, which was published, tellingly, on April Fool's Day 2002:

> I've got the best job in the world. What would your boss do if he or she caught you taking a leisurely wander around Victoria Beckham's home on her website or leading your colleagues in a discussion of what the future might hold for Kat Slater during working hours? You'd get told off – I'd probably get promoted.
>
> It seems like a complete blag that I have managed to find a profession in which my passions for celebrity, TV and popular culture are not only indulged but are requirements of the job. I work at *Heat* and people's fascination with celebrity has led to us becoming the magazine with the fastest-growing circulation in Europe. And it's so much fun, sometimes I can't believe they actually pay me for it. But a year into the job, I have discovered that there is, of course, a catch. I don't know if it happened when I was writing about Kylie's bum, Brooklyn's toys or Sarah Jessica Parker's wardrobe, but it appears that I have caught celebrity. Not fame, just celebrity – and believe me, the two things are different.

It never occurred to me that if you are constantly writing about another, more privileged life, you eventually start to expect it for yourself. In my case, the symptoms of star-syndrome began to manifest themselves slowly but steadily over time.

I can understand that you now probably harbour a desire to punch Polly in the mouth should you ever meet her (she'll be easy to recognize – the smug one) but I can assure you, she's no exception. There isn't a sports writer who's managed an England team, let alone kicked a ball in anger for one, there isn't a music journalist who's recorded a platinum album and the list of Academy Award-nominated film critics is inestimably small. Indeed, even the one and only quality you'd expect to find with any certainty – an ability to write – is often conspicuous by its absence. There are many journalists earning a living writing for the papers and magazines you read every day who can hardly string a sentence together. They rely on the media's thought police, the subs or production editors, to turn their verbiage into readable prose.

Jeremy Derbyshire, a senior sports reporter with several years experience, sent the following email to his editor. Jeremy now works for a national mid-market tabloid and this is a verbatim copy of an email he sent to his editor Simon Kerslake requesting a day off work. I suppose you might think I've made this up, or that I was tempted to add a couple of extra typos, but please believe me – I didn't have to.

```
From:      Jeremy Derbyshire
Sent:      20 April 2000 16:27
To:        Simon Kerslake
Subject:   None

Simon,
Everything is in place for next weeks
ireland match, I should be ablle to get
plent y out of it news wise and interview
wisr so i think it will be well worh it.
I want to be there on Monday evening when
the squad assambles in Dublin so I was
wondring if i could have Monday of so I
could spend Easter at home.
If there is not enough to cover on Monday
i will understand but it would aslso help
me get what I need.

Cheers Jez
```

It's not Oscar Wilde, is it? Yet, just like Oscar, Jez makes a living from his skill with the written word.

Yet, by dint of their profession, all of these people – unlike you – will be enjoying the trappings of stardom. Like the celebrities they write about, they'll be travelling first class, getting free things on a daily basis and enjoying the kind of life that you can only read about. And why? Well, it all comes back to that £2.5 billion PR spend we talked about in the previous chapter. A little over 70% of all public relations effort is focused on what is known as marketing public relations, or product promotion. There are really only two ways that products can be promoted through public relations. The first is through straightforward media relations, in which PRs try to convince journalists to write about the product either in review sections or as the basis of a feature. The second is by association or intervention, usually through a stunt or third-party/celebrity endorsement. The tactics employed vary from press briefings, conferences and one-to-ones to press releases, offering pre-written features or case studies, product sampling and media packs at trade shows. The process may be simple; the problem is that there's a heck of a lot of product competing for the space. Journalists receive mountains of what is, essentially, crap. PRs, whose approach is usually to scatter-gun to as many journalists as possible through as many channels as possible usually post, email, phone and fax. As a result, journalists waste hours wading through stuff that isn't relevant to them. And now the punchline arrives: because of this, they then have to field hundreds of calls from PRs who ring to ask if they've received the release/email/fax and who continue to try to persuade them that this new egg whisk really is of interest to the readers of *What Laptop*.

PRs view journalists as no more than a conduit to coverage in the magazine. There isn't a PR in practice who wouldn't rather just write the copy themselves. For some reason, society in general puts great store by what critics say about a film, CD, video game, product or motor car. There are exceptions, but good reviews and notices, while not guaranteeing success, play an enormous helping hand.

In truth, most of us know that a critic's opinion is no more valid than our own. It is far easier to manage a football team from the press box than it is from the dugout, and nobody suggested sacking the football editor of the *Sun* for incorrectly insisting that Edgar Davids had signed for Chelsea. Yet our desire to fit in, to make the right decision, to be informed, is well served by the Everyman opinions expressed in the pages of the national and specialist press, and so the symbiotic relationship between press and PRs continues. The PR's clients want positive opinion; the PR does their best to extract an appropriate opinion from the journalist and the journalist helps himself to another dozen oysters and a glass of Moët & Chandon, insisting that their opinion can't be bought and that the readers must come first.

Much of this book is unashamed opinion, but among the polemic there are one or two facts, and here's one of them: if opinions couldn't be bought, then £2.5 billion wouldn't have been spent on PR last year.

Most journalists quickly become accustomed to being treated to the high life; they enjoy being beneficiaries of corporate plastic on press trips and junkets. Why review the gig in Windsor when we can fly you to the show in New York? Fancy test-driving the new car – can you be in Indonesia next week? Feeling cold? Have a promotional *Lord of the Rings* cloak on us. The receipt of this largesse can have an interesting effect on the journalist's personality. If the City Slacker within awakens, the job becomes more about jollies than journalism, inevitably linked to a phenomenal growth in the perception of their own opinion. Hubris.

For PRs this kind of journalistic self-belief becomes an occupational hazard, and dealing with it an inherent function of the job. Tom Baker (not the famous *Doctor Who* actor, the less famous video games critic) was not an unpleasant fellow but unfortunately (for him), provides a very colourful example of just this kind of City Slacker. My first meeting with Tom came three days into my new job as PR manager for a video games publisher. The launch of the company's pillar title had been planned months before my arrival and due to a spurious link with pizzas, and some geographical reasons I still don't understand, I was dispatched to Pizza Express in Oxford to attend the launch party. The marketing director regarded this as an excellent opportunity for me to get to know the press.

The event was due to start at 2pm, a buffet of pizza (what else?) and champagne had been laid on and after a sociable preamble, the media pack would be taken through to a presentation suite. There they would be given a detailed demonstration of the product and, once fully convinced of its genius, would be dispatched with review code and obligatory promotional T-shirt and baseball jacket. Partly due to the fact that none of the invited magazines were actually based in Oxford but in a variety of locations across the UK, and partly due to the vagaries of the rail network, our 15 invitees did not arrive all at once. By 2pm, the four members of our marketing team had been joined by a production assistant from a TV production company and a freelance journalist from a local radio station. The hot buffet was getting cold and the champagne was now not so much on ice as in lukewarm water.

It's fair to say that the conversation was strained. We'd covered "Where have you come from/did you have any trouble finding the place/please help yourself to some pizza" and were now sitting in a rather uncomfortable silence. There was a lot of looking at watches and curling of toes but very little in the way of chit-chat or even eye contact. The silence continued and in these circumstances, ten minutes can seem like an eternity. Here were six people thrown together by circumstance, with nothing to say to each other. Four of us (the marketing department) may have been wondering how we were going to explain the poor turnout back at HQ, but collectively we were all hoping – no, praying – that somebody, anybody, would simply say something. Just as long as it wasn't me.

At 2.14pm Tom Baker arrived, a large jolly figure dressed in what can only be described as a computer games reviewer's outfit: jeans, *Sonic the Hedgehog* promotional leather jacket and *Red Dwarf* T-shirt. "Hi everyone, sorry I'm late. I'm Tom from *PC Games Review*!" announced Tom. We didn't care where he was from; he'd broken the silence and we were all human beings, after all. As the group seized on this crumb of humanity, we all loved Tom and his unforced jolliness and we all wanted to hear what he had to say. Tom was shown to a seat and asked where he came from/did he have any trouble finding the place/would he like to help himself to some pizza? Alas, having exhausted our conversational store cupboard, the seven of us quickly sank back into the now-familiar, but still uncomfortable, silence. But Tom was not giving up so quickly. Polishing off his slice of cold American pizza, he addressed the group quizzically: "Did anyone see *Star Trek: Next Generation* last night?" Now, I'm not a fan of *Star Trek*, but after nearly 13 minutes of stony silence I was dying to find out what had happened during last night's episode to ... not Kirk but the other one, who used to be in the Royal Shakespeare Company. Evidently, the rest of the group shared my desire. We looked askance at each other. No, it was clear that none of us had seen last night's episode of *Star Trek: Next Generation*, so please Tom, tell us pray, what on earth happened? "Oh I didn't see it either," said a very disappointed Tom, "I just wondered if anyone else had." At that point the marketing manager decided to give up on small talk and press on with the presentation. It was either that or give up on life and I still respect him for his decision.

Over the next few years I got to know Tom as a supremely opinionated reviewer. Seemingly stuck in an eternal bridesmaid role of section editor without ever being considered for promotion, he was barely to be found in the office, spending at least 50% of his time travelling the globe to look at unfinished computer games and write about them. What set Tom apart was not so much this but his behaviour whenever he received a game for review. For the most part, getting early review scores out of reviewers is a futile exercise. The reviewer has nothing to gain. If it's a bad review, you might throw your rattle out of the pram and pull your advertising in a futile attempt to overturn the mark. If they only tell you when you've got a good review, you can deduce that when they won't tell you anything, your product must have got a bad one and again rattles and advertising can be thrown and pulled. If it happened to be Tom reviewing your game, however, it was a different matter. It was impossible to get him off the phone. He'd ring up with a blow-by-blow account of exactly where the designer had gone wrong and email a 3,000-word proposal for improvements in the sequel, regardless of the fact that the review itself was just 600 words long. He'd want to talk to the producer, the game designer, tester, creative director, MD, security guard – in fact, anyone willing to listen – and would happily tell them that two years of their life had been wasted because he could tell after just an hour or so of playing it *exactly* where they'd gone wrong. The good news was that he was only too happy to make sure that they didn't make the same mistakes in the next one. To my knowledge, no one ever took Tom up on one of his generous offers but there was one moment, in a bar on a memorable press trip, when Tom was able to summarize his proposition beautifully:

> The thing is, Steve, I've spent nearly ten years playing computer games which consistently disappoint in one way or another. I get paid for my opinion and I reckon I've played almost every game that's ever come out. What amazes me is that no one has ever offered me a job as a games designer – with all my experience, I'm sure I'd be brilliant at it.

Applying Tom's theory to my own unique talent, I'm equally amazed that nobody has offered me a film deal or indeed the opportunity to record a solo album, as I've seen hundreds of films and listened to thousands of albums, and I can certainly tell a good one when I see or hear it. The only two things stopping me are talent and musical ability. Maybe it's the same with Tom.

As the journalist slacker begins to take the trappings of their job for granted, it's easy for them to get carried away with the fact that many of them really don't have any special talent at all, just a propensity to be in the right place at the right time. At times, the role of PRs can feel more like a teacher on a school trip than a spin doctor.

On an all-expenses paid press junket, it's not unusual for journalists to leave wallets and brains at home. Neil Evans, who now works as a senior PR adviser to a leading software company, recalled the time that he took a group of senior technology editors to a European product launch in Versailles. One of the press pack was Tony Kelly, the gargantuan 25-stone editor of a leading home electronics title. Over the years I'd had several run-ins with Tony, who is the kind of person – a bit like Ann Robinson – about whom you never hear anyone say something non-committal about: everybody hated him. On one trip (just for a laugh) he'd emptied his minibar, running up a £280 bill on beer nuts and small tins of Heineken for which, needless to say, the PR picked up the tab. On this particular occasion, however, Tony did it to himself. Disembarking at Paris Charles de Gaulle Airport, he was asked by customs officials if there was anything in his bag. "Only a bomb!" he replied, smiling with those big sausage lips of his. The smile disappeared shortly afterwards as he was frogmarched into a secure room and subjected to the kind of rigorous body search that the Chilean Military Police would describe as "overzealous".

Then enjoying a spell as England manager, Kevin Keegan was the talent behind a product launch being handled by another PR, Martin Congreve. Martin had put his client's two hours of precious Keegan time to good use, arranging a dozen "exclusive" interviews in ten-minute slots across a good mix of broadcast, national and lifestyle press. On the day of the event, Martin took a frantic phone call from magazine editor Trevor Barker. Due to a family bereavement, Trevor explained, he would be unable to attend in person, but was eager to transfer his press accreditation to his staff writer Tarquin Hindmarsh. Martin was happy to oblige, being very keen to confirm his front cover, but he did have some reservations about Tarquin, who cut an unlikely figure as a style magazine journalist in his Wolverhampton Wanderers shirt and bojangles jewellery. With a reputation for not knowing one end of a Dictaphone from another, Martin had always assumed that Tarquin was related to some member of senior management. "Don't worry," Trevor assured him, sensing his concern, "I've given him a set of questions, so all he has to do is turn the Dictaphone on and read them out loud."

The interviews were taking place at the Bank of England sports ground in Richmond, i.e. miles from anywhere. Tarquin arrived, as expected, in his Wolves shirt with a carrier bag containing everything he needed (a Dictaphone and scrappy list of questions), looking every inch the next John Pilger. His second question to Martin (after "Is there a free bar?") was: "Do you know where I can get some batteries for my Dictaphone? I think these are a bit flat." Without too much trouble Martin managed to source a spare set from a better-prepared hack and directed

Tarquin to the bar. When his slot finally came, Martin ushered him from the bar, explaining that no, it probably wouldn't be OK if he took his red wine with him and took him in for his ten-minute interview with the by-then rather tired England manager.

Kevin Keegan is nothing if not a "people person" and, despite a rather gruelling schedule, he was happy to make small talk while Tarquin got himself sorted. Keegan clocked the Wolves shirt and commented that he'd actually been a Wolves fan himself as a child. He explained that they were the Manchester United of their day (that day apparently being sometime in the 1950s). As Tarquin fumbled with batteries, Dictaphone and crumpled list of questions, talk turned to Billy Wright, the first ever floodlit match with the Hungarian team Kispest Honvéd, Willie Carr's free kick and the sleeping giant's chances of a top flight return under the aegis of Sir Jack Hayward.

After five minutes of chat, now firmly established as Wolves' number one fan and with his Dictaphone finally running, Tarquin started reading Trevor's questions out. It was clear this wasn't going to be a forensic interview in the style of Jeremy Paxman or John Humphrys. To give you an idea, a playback would have sounded like this.

Tarquin: Right Kevin, thanks for giving up the time to speak to us today.

Kevin Keegan: That's no problem.

Tarquin: First of all then, what impact do you think the Premiership is having on the smaller clubs in the league like my own club, Torquay United?

Kevin Keegan: [confused] ???

Tarquin: [starts to repeat question, assuming Keegan hasn't heard him] What impact ...

Kevin Keegan: [still confused] On *your* club Torquay United? I thought you were a Wolves fan?

Tarquin: [holding up sheet] It says Torquay United on here.

At least that's what a playback would have sounded like if Tarquin had actually recorded the interview. A further 30 seconds in and voices started to come out of the Dictaphone, thus making it clear he'd pressed "play" rather than "record". These days you'll find Tarquin editing a national monthly entertainment magazine and his work regularly appears in two leading broadsheets.

On a footballing theme, the editor of a new football magazine was invited by a colleague of mine at Umbro to attend that Saturday's match between Tottenham and Chelsea. "What time's kick-off?" he famously replied.

The ability to get everything for free has a naturally corrupting influence. I've worked with a number of professional footballers over the years – some charming, some pig ignorant – all of whom have had two things in common. First, they've all earned in a week the kind of money that Chris Tarrant doesn't want to give you on *Who Wants To Be A Millionaire*. Second, they've been desperate to get their hands on whatever free T-shirts, CDs or DVDs we've been plugging, with a net value to the client of around 50p.

Journalist City Slackers suffer the same malaise: first out of the taxi and last into the bar. Ben Thompson was a notorious freeloader. During a meal out one evening with a group of ten journalists, Martin Congreve bought one of the other editors a packet of cigarettes. From the look on Ben's face he could see that he was seriously thinking about starting smoking in order to take advantage of the free fags on offer. On press trips Ben would ritually empty his hotel room of anything that wasn't nailed down; on one embarrassing occasion he was forced to hand back an ashtray he'd pilfered at the checkout (as I said, *seriously* thinking about starting smoking). Ben's freeloading wasn't unique, but what did mark him out from the herd was his brazen way of, well, asking for things. One time I was invited to an album launch party by a friend of mine who was head of marketing at a record label. Completely unconnected to me in any way, Ben and his colleagues from the magazine found themselves at the same party. Upon entering, he made his way across to my table: "What's the score with the bar?" Ben asked, "Is it free?"

"I think it's free up until 8pm, but then you have to pay," I replied as helpfully as I could.

"Right," said Ben, nodding in understanding. "And after that, you pay for them, yeah?"

On another occasion during a press trip to LA, Ben retired to bed early after a convivial evening in the hotel bar. Evidently thinking that his early departure called his rock-and-roll credentials into question, he joined us for breakfast, looking slightly the worse for wear. "Sorry I'm late, guys," he explained. "I got back to the room last night and went a bit ape. I trashed the mini-bar, tore through the porn, fell asleep on the floor with my boots on and woke up this morning ... Sick everywhere. I was hammered. Sorry, Steve." Mildly concerned that this unexpected beano would appear on my company credit card, I took the liberty of checking Ben's tab with reception on the way back to my room. It read:

Mini bar item: Can of Coke	$2.40
In-room movie: *Men In Black*	$10.95

Not everyone gets away with it. City Slackers walk a line where it's OK to take liberties along the way; in some senses it's expected, but occasionally – just occasionally – they do get their comeuppance.

I was planning to go for a drink with an old college friend, Andy Melton, who was editing a DVD magazine. He was on deadline but figured he'd be finished by 5.30pm, so we arranged to meet at his office then before hooking up with the rest of the group a couple of hours later. When I arrived, things didn't seem to be going that well. Kev, the usually chipper production editor, had a face like thunder and the rest of the staff who should have been winding down were a blur of activity. Andy explained that he was running a bit late due to that fact that the issue – which should have gone to the printer at 5.30pm that evening – was 23 pages short, 17 of which were the responsibility of Carl, the deputy editor. I noticed that Carl was absent from the scene. To cut a long story short, Andy had returned from holiday to find that his (soon to be former) deputy had accepted a seven-day press trip to the US without authorization and with 17 out of his 18 pages of monthly copy quota as yet unwritten. Missives from the US had been unforthcoming, so the rest of the magazine staff was now having to drum up two weeks' work in about 45 minutes.

Andy was clearly not coming out to play, but rather than wait in the pub on my own, I decided to watch a DVD in a quiet corner of the office before sloping off to meet the rest of the group. About 1 hour, 15 minutes and 25 seconds into a time-coded version of *The Day After Tomorrow*, Kev the production editor wandered across.

"Is that any good?" he asked.

"Oh, it's not bad. Not really my kind of thing, but you know …"

"Great. You don't fancy knocking out a 500-word review, do you?"

The biggest dilemma for journalist slackers is one of remuneration or, more to the point, the lack of it. True, the giants of "Me" journalism – the Will Selfs, Jeremy Clarksons, AA Gills and Julie Burchills of this world – will all be pulling basic salaries well in excess of six figures, while many of the relative minnows (and even some of the actual minnows) will be hoping to emulate the televisual success of former literary giants like Kate Thornton. But for most, eking out a living in the page of small consumer titles, the salaries will be modest. Career progression is another issue. In the publishing world, editorial staff will always be well and truly on the cost side of the balance sheet, to be trimmed in ebbing times. Rising through the ranks to the giddy heights of editor may not take too long for the talented, but from here to who knows where. The career options for an editor in their late 20s or early 30s are limited to say the least: another magazine perhaps, the excitement but uncertainty of a new launch or a step over into the dark side of PR or publishing, a world of suits and spreadsheets. The alternative is to stay with the magazine, another *Groundhog Day* of "the same but different" publication month in, month out, until the inevitable closure happens. It's an option many take: the now-defunct BBC football magazine *Match of the Day* had only one member of staff leave in the three years prior to its closure.

Perhaps inevitably, as the gloss of free bars and press trips gives way to the realities of mortgages and families, our bright young things can transform into cynical old things. There are precious few journalists over 35 who would concur with Polly Hudson's statement that they've got the best job in the world.

For many, writing is not an end in itself, but a means: vicarious membership of the modern cult of celebrity and the possibility of hosting a panel show on digital TV. Many decide to forgo the salaried world to pursue a freelance career, lured by the opportunity to work from home writing case studies and reports for corporate clients who have to pay over the odds for a report written by the ex-editor of *X* magazine. At every industry trade show you'll find them walking the floors, networking, pressing business cards into the hands of contacts, eager to discuss the possibility of providing the copy for this year's annual report or corporate brochure. A couple of years ago, I was at a trade show in Olympia when the former editor of a national film magazine arrived on the stand. He'd resigned after five years in the job and, after taking 12 months' sabbatical, was ready to plunge himself into the freelance world. He'd had enough of editing and wanted to get back to his first love: writing. He handed me a business card: if I was looking for someone to do a better job of the company brochure, then he was the man, competitive rates, just give him a call. We shook hands as he left the stand and I promised to keep in touch even though, I'm ashamed to say, I didn't. I looked at the business card. It said:

Tom Price
Freelance Writer

Journalism at it's best.

8 | Computer Says "No!"

Old joke corner: "There are only 10 kinds of people in the world: there are those who understand binary and those who don't."

A computer now sits on virtually every desk in every office in the western world and most of them are connected to virtually every other computer in every office in the western world. The permeation of technology into every aspect of work and home life has taken little more than 20 years, yet today we find it hard to imagine how the world functioned without it. Those of us old enough to remember the emergence of home computers in the 1980s – the ZX Spectrum, BBC Micro, Commodore 64 et al. – will be able to recall a time not all that long ago when there was no "e" or "snail" variants, there was simply "mail"; a time when the fastest way of getting photos or artwork across the country was on the back of a motorbike.

The hardware infrastructure provided by personal computers, personal digital assistants (PDAs), telecom networks and the internet has driven in turn the demand for functionality or software. In order to maintain, support and improve the myriad of different computer systems, IT networks and software products, an army of IT specialists, programmers, analysts, software engineers, web designers and project managers have found gainful employment. Furthermore, despite the dot.com crash, the high-performing stocks on the world's equity markets are still those of the "spend today, profit tomorrow" technology companies. This kind of hi-tech company needs to raise capital to fund the development of products and services that promise to be at the very heart of tomorrow's world. Maybe. The result is they often have price to earnings, or P/E, ratios that have little to do with their ability to generate revenue today, but plenty to do with the opinions of non-expert investors.

To some extent, every modern business is reliant on the expertise provided by IT specialists. Even companies that ply their trade far away from the shiny world of hi-tech will run software on computers that will require, once they reach a certain size, the supervision of a dedicated IT manager or team. Invest in the creation of a website and, who knows, maybe an intranet or extranet, some viral marketing, a better web connection, servers, video conferencing, voice IP, PDA software for fieldworkers ... Before you know it, your business has become reliant on this white magic that you don't really understand. At first you will wonder how you ever survived without it, but rest assured: in 18 months' time you will be wondering why everything is running so slowly. Time to upgrade. No doubt the investment made under the auspices of replacing old-fashioned and inefficient paper-based systems handled by Janice on reception will save the company time and money, making it better able to compete in the new world global economic order. But that's probably enough about technology. I'm definitely the kind of person who doesn't understand binary (so if anyone does get that joke at the beginning of the chapter, please email me) but I'm in good company, because neither does about 98.5% of the world's population.

This is obviously excellent news for IT specialists, and for me goes a long way to explaining why the dot.com bubble burst in the spectacular way that it did. In 2000* Paul Lewis, like many others, had listened to the advice of the experts and abandoned a promising career in the "old economy" to make his fortune in the exciting world of e-commerce. Six months into the job, he was beginning to get really concerned about how quickly his company was burning through its seed capital and was finding it a real struggle to make sense of the business plan. A timely networking opportunity presented itself. One of Paul's friends from his former company invited him for an evening of corporate hospitality at the World Rugby League play-off between St Helens and Brisbane. This was an opportunity for Paul to get his digital solutions business in front of 12 potential clients so, of course, he jumped at the chance.

The match was excellent (with Saints the surprise winners, courtesy of a last-minute try) but the networking event ended up being far more important for his business than Paul could have possibly imagined. There were representatives from 12 companies present. Each company was at a different stage of development; some were starting up, some were looking for second-round funding while others had already achieved a flotation on the stock market. What they had in common was, first of all, that they were all technology companies; second, that none of

---

*Which still sounds like the future to me.

them was making any money. The whole room was exchanging business cards and the atmosphere was very friendly, but it quickly became apparent to Paul that everybody was trying desperately to sell to everybody else in the room. Over the next few months, Paul would attend a number of meetings where both sides were trying to sell to each other, but this was his first real exposure to the phenomenon. Here were 12 products, each one looking for a market and, in 11 cases, failing to find it.

Launching new products is fraught with risk. In 2002 almost 25,000 brand new items were unleashed on the market, and while there were obviously a few hits, most appeared fleetingly on the shelves before being abruptly withdrawn forever, forgotten even by the people that conceived them. The brief history of the web is littered with services that no one has asked for and sites that no one has visited. For example, Clickmango.com allowed you to get health foods and vitamins delivered straight to your door; Boo.com spent a fortune ensuring that all three of its customers could get real-time individualized style advice in seven different languages from an animated character. Moonfruit.com allowed you to create your own website for free; while at flutter.com you could pretend to be a bookmaker and set your own odds. In all these and countless other instances, the companies behind them were driven by innovation, "blue-sky" opportunity or exploring the art of the possible. But while their products were, no doubt, pushing back some technological boundary or other, nobody stopped to consider the answer to the big question of the day: so what?

Today, technological invention is the mother of product development, and modern inventors are more likely to be found behind computers in the air-conditioned offices of R&D departments than they are in the potting shed. In 2001 IBM successfully secured over 3,000 patents, a record number; more than 1,500 were for infrastructure technologies such as software, servers and storage systems. It is widely understood that consumers don't buy technology, but functionality. There are few people who fully understand how even basic utilities like electricity work*; the fact that it's always there whenever we need it, providing light, heat, hot water and digital television, is taken for granted. Yet often the very same non-technical people can be found running companies or departments that rely, either wholly or for the most part, on the smooth running of equipment and systems about which they have little or no understanding. The situation is very similar to taking your car in for a service and being confronted with a £500 bill for "essential parts". Unless you're a mechanic yourself, you're unlikely to be able to say with any certainty whether anyone even opened the bonnet, let alone whether any work was carried out. And if it was, to what standard it was completed.

In many ways, IT services work on exactly the same principle. IT support can be invisible in an organization, and when things are going smoothly, it generally is. But if the server crashes, email fails or internet connectivity is

---

*And the answer isn't: "By turning on a switch on the wall."

147

lost, there will be an immediate call to action from everyone affected. Heads will be shaken, tempers will be frayed and the competence of the IT support team will be called into question; but once the fault is rectified, everyone will forget all about them until the next time that things go wrong. One thing is inevitable: that no one will be given a satisfactory reason as to why the fault happened in the first place.

To a man – and they are almost always men – techie City Slackers revel in this civilian lack of understanding. Put what you consider to be a perfectly legitimate question to a Techie Slacker and you'll be greeted with incomprehensible jargon delivered in a manner suggesting that you are being told the obvious. If there is more than one of them present in the room when you ask this question, they'll wink knowingly at each other, as if to say: "We know which one of the 10 kinds of people you are."

Civilian: "Why hasn't the new version of the company website been updated? I thought it was going live this morning."

Techie Slacker: "Have you emptied your cache?"

Civilian: "What's that?"

Techie Slacker: "It's the pages stored in your web browser."

Civilian: "And if I do that will I see the new website?"

Techie Slacker: "Yes."

Civilian: "Are you sure most of our customers will know how to do this?"

Techie Slacker: "Yes."

[After five minutes, the cache is duly located and emptied, but there's still no website.]

Civilian: "Hi, it's me again, I've emptied the cache but I'm still getting the old version."

Techie Slacker: "What version of Explorer are you using?"

Civilian: "Erm, how do I find that out?"

[A brief explanation follows.]

Civilian: "Right. It's 4.1."

Techie Slacker: "You need 4.2, you'll have to download it from the Microsoft website."

Civilian: "How do I do that?"

[A brief explanation follows. Version 4.2 is downloaded, but still no website.]

Civilian: "Still no joy, I'm afraid."

Techie Slacker: "Right, it'll take a while to propagate around the internet, you must be pointing at a server that hasn't propagated yet. Give us a call at the end of the day if it's still not up and we'll have a look at your machine."

Civilian: "Actually, I'm now a bit concerned. We've spent

several hundred thousand pounds advertising the launch of the new website today and I'm worried that people are simply not going to be able to find it."

Techie Slacker: "Don't worry, it'll only affect about 5% of them, you're just unlucky. Unless they've got a Mac, where it won't work at all …"

A simplistic example perhaps, but one that I am sure will resonate with anyone who has had to commission a technical product or service. As I said, I am not what you would call technically minded, and perhaps I'm naive to expect these things to work in the same way that electricity does, by flicking a switch. This analogy provides a neat segue into a story told to me recently by someone who is technically minded. Gary Jones is a senior project manager at one of the world's biggest software solutions providers. His job is to run a large team of programmers and software engineers who collectively provide power management solutions for many of the world's leading electricity generators. Gary is something of an expert in the field of power management and although this perhaps lacks the cachet of being say, a stuntman, test pilot or bus conductor, it is obviously a highly important job and I am proud to call the man who runs the team that makes sure my light comes on when I flick the switch my friend.

The company is huge, employing over 5,000 people. Most of these employees are engaged in project work for similarly huge, blue-chip clients. The demands of the job mean there is occasionally some downtime. Between projects Gary and his team spend much of their time surfing the internet, playing Counter-Strike and trading on eBay*. But when a big project comes in, deadlines are tight: 14-hour days and seven-day weeks are the norm.

First, the biggest problem Gary faces is that software systems are now so big, it is impossible to build anything from scratch. Instead, new modules are plugged into the existing system. So far so good – except that the pace of technological change is so great, parts of the systems that he's plugging his latest wizardry into might as well have been written in fingerpaint during the Stone Age. Second, writing code is a much more personal experience that 98.5% of us might imagine. Asking a coder to finish off someone else's program is a bit like asking them to finish off someone else's essay in the same handwriting. Finally, the personal nature of the job means there is plenty of scope for ego, so when, as you might expect, you do ask someone to finish off someone else's program, they will react in the same way that electricians do when they survey the mess that the last bloke made of rewiring your house.

The upshot is that if something does go wrong (which occasionally it does), finding out what the problem is, and who is responsible for it, requires the detective expertise of Miss Marple. Ask a straight question and you'll find yourself stonewalled, as the programming team responds with a collective "Not us" while hiding its individually

---

*According to Gary, there are several people on the same floor as him but not in his team (I hasten to add) who, judging by their behaviour, seem to have been "between projects" for the past two or three years.

responsible heads behind *Buffy the Vampire Slayer* magazines and network games of Warcraft.

Apparently, one of the most important aspects of power management is matching the supply to demand. I was aware that there is allegedly a power surge as kettles are turned on during the ad break on *Coronation Street*, but frankly I was unaware that in order to legislate for the multiple cups of tea, someone at the power station has to increase output accordingly, drawing any additional power required from elsewhere in the grid. Nowadays, that someone has been replaced by a computer system and in the particular case of one leading power company a few years ago, by a computer system that got its plusses and minuses mixed up. This minor oversight on behalf of the programmer, which hadn't been picked up during over 2,000 hours of testing, meant that on the day that the system went live, just as everyone decided the second half of their favourite soap would be much better enjoyed with a mug of hot tea, the system noted the increased demand for output and promptly shut down the power, plunging several regions into temporary darkness.

Techies are often regarded as highly intelligent people, when in truth they just know a little bit more about an unfamiliar subject than the rest of the people with whom they're working. The British have never had much time for intellectuals, preferring a deep-seated faith in the values of commonsense. Suspicious of experts and "jargon", at its best this attitude can produce a healthy scepticism about ideas, ideologies and false promises. The downside is that it can sell people short radically, and in its populist forms can lead to the celebration of the puerile, like Jade Goody from *Big Brother*, *Heat* magazine, Westlife and Jordan. In the business world, this means that attitudes to techies are polarised. In some businesses their opinions carry far too much weight while in others, no one listens to them at all. It is very difficult to find any middle ground, which explains why typically, technology itself is either viewed as a panacea or as the devil incarnate.

There are numerous examples of companies operating a successful product-led strategy, where products are developed for an as-yet undefined or immature market. It's certainly more exciting than carrying out research into the kinds of products that the market wants and then trying to develop them. Companies inspired to follow this kind of strategy tend to hold up Sony, Microsoft or even BT as role models without paying lip service to the fact that these organizations' R&D departments themselves are held up by billions of dollars of profit from existing well-defined revenue streams.

There are plenty of can-do operators with brilliant applications for PC, 3G mobile, PDA or other platforms that promise to outperform the market leader, revolutionize their particular sector and save their clients millions. Unfortunately, IT managers like to buy products from companies that aren't going to go out of business in the next six months, and while these people might not know much about technology, they do know it never works as well as the company selling it claims it will. Hi-tech companies can go out of business not because their product isn't any good – although it definitely isn't as good as they think it is – but because, by and large, no one wants to take a risk unless they have to; they know it's the second mouse that gets the cheese. Consequently Janice, who is operating the current paper-based system, doesn't look like she's going anywhere in the near future. The opportunity to make a sale often depends more on providence than on planning, and if they do manage to make a sale, the Techie Slacker knows that the value is not in what the product cost to make, but in what their client thinks it's worth and how much they're prepared to pay for it.

Back in 2000, with the networking event widely regarded as a limited failure, Paul Lewis, along with his fellow directors, was busily re-engineering his business. An opportunity had emerged for him to create an online football quiz game for one of his clients. Looking at the budget and list of deliverables, Paul could see that it was going to be difficult to make the numbers stack up. The client had £30,000 to spend and using some clever arithmetic, Paul felt that he could manage to bring it in for only £29,550. While the margin was nothing to write home about, at that time any turnover was gratefully received, so the board decided to do it.

When it was finally launched, the product proved quite a success, exceeding the expectations of the client who was, no doubt, as pleased with the paltry price they'd paid for it as they were with the performance of the game itself. A few months later, with the company finally starting to turn around, Paul took a call from a large mobile handset company who were looking to get involved in football. They had commissioned some research which had picked up Paul's game on his client's website and wanted to know if he could create a similar version for them. Paul arrived at the meeting with his sales director, both of whom were fully availed of all the information. Having spoken to the technical and content teams they were confident that they could do this version for much less than the original. Running the figures through a spreadsheet on the way to the meeting, they were able to conclude that if they reused the engine, polished up the graphics and offered a little bit more functionality, then rather than the three months that it had taken to do the first version, version 2 would take just under three weeks and would cost only £5,800. This obviously left them with a much healthier margin than they'd secured for version 1.

At the meeting, things were going well until the client came to the subject of money. Funds were limited, he explained, the game was great, but they didn't want to be too exposed here, how much would it cost? Paul's heart sank, but before he could mumble something about wanting at least £25,000 to deliver it by the end of the month his sales director, in an act of supreme brinkmanship, stated calmly: "It'll take three months and cost you £250,000." And it did.

The point is: when it was finally launched the product proved quite a success, exceeding the expectations of the client who was, no doubt, as pleased with the paltry price that they'd paid for it as they were with the performance of the game itself. Both companies are household names and both had paid what they thought was a fair price for essentially the same product. In both cases Paul's strategy had been simply to charge as much as he could; but in the second instance he had been able to command a premium because this client happened to have a much bigger problem to solve.

This strategy to pricing extends throughout the service sector. How much does a website cost? It depends who you ask. Lloyds TSB paid an around £15 million for theirs; whether they got value for money rather depends on whether their supplier saw them as the kind of company that understands binary (£30,000) or the kind that doesn't (£250,000), and how desperate they were for the work.

Shortly after the quiz triumph, Paul was invited over to Neon, Switzerland to pitch for the UEFA website. His company really wanted the business and committed several weeks' work to the unpaid tender. The team pulled out all the stops, creating an impressive prototype supported with a detailed breakdown of costs. Paul worked on the assumption that this was a company that understood binary and pitched in with a price that was tight but certainly deliverable. He rang the office from the airport with a progress report. They had been the second last company in to pitch, the presentation had gone swimmingly and, on the way out, the marketing director had tipped him the wink that they were going to get it. By the time he landed at Manchester Airport, it was all over. The final company in to pitch had offered to do the site for nothing on the grounds that announcing UEFA as a client would generate additional business for them and act as a loss leader. What struck me about their approach was not so much the fact that they'd won the account, but the fact that had they gone in with a nominal cost of £50,000 or even £100,000, the net effect would have been the same: they'd have won the business. Unless, of course, they knew something that Paul didn't – perhaps they had lost business in the past to a similar strategy. Like the networking event nine months earlier, the loss proved something of a watershed for Paul. If the prize for being the last man standing is a bag of balloons, what's the point in entering the competition? He exited the digital solutions market shortly afterwards.

One interesting trait exemplified by all Techie Slackers, but especially those engaged in software development, is one associated more often with exponents of the traditional creative arts. If you ever meet a serious musician, no matter how famous they are, they may well ask you how you enjoyed the show or what you thought of their latest album. It is always tempting to see this as an invitation to provide a slice of helpfully constructive criticism, but be assured: if you suggest that you found their oeuvre even marginally less impressive than *Sergeant Pepper*, they may smile and thank you for your comments, but they will secretly want to kill you.

Similarly, even the shabbiest games development team in Christendom believes that its current working title will eclipse the populist appeal of *Tomb Raider*. Software engineers working on a graphic user interface for the local garage's website will share anecdotes about the poor quality of the coding in Office 2000. In fact, don't take my word for it – take theirs. Here are just a few postings taken from some of the countless techie news groups and forums online:

SUBJECT: Why is Windows so bad?

"I was discussing this point with a friend of mine last night. First, a little background. We are both IT professionals. Windows has some weaknesses that make it terrible for a home environment. It does take a lot of expertise to administer a Windows computer. The user interface in Windows is terrible. File management is a nightmare."

SUBJECT: Why Half-Life is lame

The one thing I don't like about Half-Life is the lame lighting effects. As soon as you turn on your torch there is a big frame rate hit, in fact any form of lighting whatsoever produces a frame rate hit. I don't remember this happening in Quake II which is using the same game engine – if the slowdown is caused by the coding of Valve then I can see why they didn't bother creating their own 3D engine from scratch, it would have rescued the game.*

SUBJECT: The dangers of using Internet Explorer

We've got CNN broadcasting how lots of folks are saying that people shouldn't use Internet Explorer. This is going to break a lot of legitimate, if badly programmed, software. (I have too many clients who bought software from lazy programmers before they met or asked me.)

When Techie Slackers are not clogging up the noticeboards and forums of the world wide web with self-satisfied comments that highlight their own ability to better the

---

*Half-Life is popularly regarded as the greatest computer game of all time.

world's most popular software packages, computer games or web browsers, often they can be found turning their attention to a much bigger question. And I'm not talking about playing Age of Empires when they're pretending to do overtime, but the very end of civilization as we know it!

Many techies claim that the biggest threat to life as we know it is not Al Qaeda, nuclear war, AIDS, famine, the war in Iraq or even George Bush, but the breakdown of something called Moore's Law (not to be confused with Murphy's Law). You may not be aware of Moore's Law yet, but you soon will be. There is plenty of discussion going on about it online: a search on Google revealed 523,000 pages, making it just over two-thirds as popular as Led Zeppelin. In December 2004 there were over 100 articles published about Moore's Law in the UK alone. All this fuss is because Moore's Law is the law that purportedly governs advances in computer technology and the development of silicon chips. It states that computer power will double every 18 months. This means that if you bought a state-of-the-art computer more than 12 months ago, the ones available today will be roughly twice as powerful. The law is pretty representative of the progress made in computing over the past 50 years, but the two big questions that it poses are bothering the techies, namely: how long can this go on for? And what happens if Moore's Law comes to an end?

In 2004 the BBC's highly-respected, long-running science magazine *Horizon* dedicated an entire programme to answering these questions. *Horizon* spoke to many leading IT experts such as City University of New York

Professor Michio Kaku, who were only too happy to put the problem into perspective. For Kaku, "The end of Moore's Law is perhaps the single greatest economic threat to modern society, and unless we deal with it we could be facing economic ruin."

I hope that got your attention and you're probably keen now to know more about Moore. Basically, the problem is silicon. To make computers run faster you need to make the chips run faster, and to make the chips run faster, you need to pack more transistors (which are like little switches) onto them. For the past 50 years, scientists have managed to double exponentially the number of these switches that they can cram onto a chip every 18 months, thus doubling the processing power of computers. Unfortunately, the number of switches that you can pack onto a chip is not infinite: silicon is made of atoms which are of a fixed size and there is a limit to how small the transistors that are made out of it can be. According to the techies, we are getting very close to reaching that finite limit and do you knows what will happen then? Fortunately for us, Professor Kaku has the answer:

"We could be facing economic stagnation because computers are simply not capable of evolving to the next step if they are based on silicon. As power levels off, the wealth of nations, the productivity of workers, the prosperity of societies, could be endangered because of the stagnation of computer power."*

---

*Source: BBC *Horizon*, 05.02.04 (The Dark Secret of Hendrik Schön).

Eek! I guess it's time to run for the hills, before the engine room of capitalism grinds to a halt, stalling economic growth and plunging our bourgeois world into chaos and darkness. No more growth, no more profit, just ruin, misery, ruin, decay, stagnation and more ruin. All you've got to look forward to is a bleak future. You'll be eating rats and selling your family for a slice of bread. In fact, why don't you just give up now?

I'm a huge fan of *Horizon*, and I see no reason to take this threat to the end of the world any less seriously than that posed in the other programmes from the series. Especially the ones by freak waves, the forthcoming ice age, global warming, super volcanoes, asteroids hitting the earth and dirty bombs. That is to say, I don't take it seriously at all. In reality, Moore's Law isn't even a law. The shadowy Moore figure behind the edict is not a scientist but Gordon E. Moore, the first CEO of Intel. Gordon says that he came up with the law in 1965, not after years of study or research but while preparing an article for *Electronics* magazine. Others claim that Moore came up with it while driving down Highway 101 in Silicon Valley. Whichever version is correct, what is true is that Moore's Law was not the result of many years' painstaking research subjected to peer review and the scrutiny of the greatest minds in his scientific field, and secondly (though in light of the previous point this hardly matters) Gordon never laid down the 18-month timeframe.

So, not a law then. A clever observation, yes, but hardly a Cassandra heralding global meltdown. For anyone able to remember as far back as the last century, the current excitement created by Moore's Law should not be too surprising. Back then, the same techie doomsayers were too wrapped up in scaring the bejeezus out of us with the last great technological threat to mankind: the millennium bug.

As 1999 clicked seamlessly into 2000, governments and corporations were left counting the cost of solving a problem that nobody was entirely sure existed in the first place. Unusually, the Russians found themselves laughing at western overreaction. The former Soviet Union had spent just $200 million on preparing for the millennium bug, which constituted less than 2% of the US budget. British Airways alone spent $420 million, compared with the $1 million spent by its Russian counterpart Aeroflot. Analysts at the Gartner Group estimated the total global spend to be a shade over $600 billion.

The debate still rages today as to whether we avoided disaster by being fantastically well prepared, or whether the Techie Slackers were responsible for the biggest scam since the South Sea Bubble. One thing is certain: the Y2K bug was a licence to print money for IT specialists. Even conservative IT analysts estimated that the US might have wasted $40 billion on the technical equivalent of a backstreet mechanic's once over: "Yup, everything's fine," he says, slamming the bonnet. "That'll be £5 million." And who are you to argue? You're too worried about Murphy's Law. Or is that Moore's Law?

To put the impact of Techie Slackers into perspective: during 2004, the UK alone wasted over £10 billion on IT projects that were not delivered, over budget or that simply unfit for their purpose. Well over half of this money came from the public sector – which is *your* hard-earned cash (or the government's easily frittered away taxes, depending on what mood you're in). This depressing reality is entirely unnecessary; much of the cost is due not to the technology itself but to endemic bad management, poor working practices and an apparent inability to learn from the mistakes of the past.

These were the conclusions of a 2004 report called "The Challenge of Complex IT Projects" by the British Computer Society and the Royal Academy of Engineering. It was particularly critical of the lack of professionalism in software engineering and computer programming, with results that are both actually dangerous and economically debilitating.

Much as Harold Wilson before him promised to build the future of the British economy on the "white heat of scientific innovation", so Tony Blair identified the hi-tech or digital industries as the producers that would fuel his government's economic strategy. Clearly, not enough of these producers are producing, but if the current output of the UK's IT industry is considered unacceptable, perhaps jobs should be advertised more honestly.

SOFTWARE ENGINEER WANTED

ROLE: You will be responsible for delivering state-of-the-art software packages, at least two years behind schedule.

RESPONSIBILITIES: You will ensure that all our

products are riddled with bugs when they reach the market, ensuring that they never work properly and will deflect all criticism with comments like: "That's not a bug, it's a feature."

Hours are nominally 9.30–6.00pm, but obviously you can pretty much do what you like during that time as no one will be checking on you. Please ensure that your line manager knows just how bad you think Windows is programmed and is kept abreast of the amendments you'd make to it.

Use jargon when speaking to non-technical staff and remember, if you can't blame any problem you encounter on the Z-Buffer, then blame it on the boogie.

Always ensure senior management understands that every product you work on is unique and couldn't be developed anywhere else in the world by anyone other that you or your team – no way!

BENEFITS: If you, or anyone else, are working later than 5.35pm, boxes of Krispy Kreme doughnuts and Domino's Pizza will be provided by the company, free of charge. If you've nothing better to do, you can always stick around playing Counter-Strike until the free food arrives.

REQUIREMENTS: The successful candidate will demonstrate an ability to consistently break deadlines, and must be able to recite the collected works of *Monty Python* verbatim. Own *Red Dwarf* T-Shirt and complete set of *Babylon 5/Deep Space 9* would be an advantage, but is not essential.

9 | Not So Tough at the Top

I began this book with a personal account of 1983. It was the year the Thatcher government won a second term that gave them, in their own minds at least, a mandate to dismantle the Keynesian machinery of successive post-war consensus governments. Thus began the process of privatization that has continued for over 20 years and has created a marketplace free of government intervention, for good or ill. Less notably, it was also the year I left school.

Ironically, given Margaret Thatcher's self-confessed admiration of the Victorian values of "toil, graft and hard work", it is this commitment to the unfettered market that has created the environmental circumstances for City Slackers to evolve; new economies, new sectors, new companies, new professions, new disciplines, new ways to hide and new weapons of mass distraction.

Among the constellation of digital TV stations – specializing in every aspect of life from extreme sports to extreme macramé – there is an unassuming channel called Challenge TV that shows reruns of classic (and not so classic) quizzes and game shows. It is from this unlikely source that I have drawn when looking for an example of this ideology from producer to City Slacker economic mindset.

Surfing the channels one evening, I stumbled across the title sequence to an edition of the long-gone darts quiz, *Bullseye*, from September 1983. I ended up watching the entire programme, which provided a vivid snapshot of the world immediately before the arrival of the City Slacker and technological revolution. By way of explanation, *Bullseye* was a pillar of early 1980s Sunday afternoon television schedules. Presented by affable northern comedian Jim Bowen, it was an attempt to capture the zeitgeist of the sporting phenomenon that was darts. Three pairs of contestants competed against each other to win big if inappropriate prizes, using a combination of general knowledge and darts-throwing skills. This unlikely formula proved a big hit for Central Television and ran for many seasons. Its catchphrases, "Your charity money's safe", "Nothing in this game for two in a bed" and "Listen to Tony", became a part of popular culture, repeated on shop floors and playgrounds throughout the country.

Two incidents from this particular episode stood out*. During the first section of the show, Jim interviews the teams and it is here we meet father and son Dave and Doug, who have came all the way from Ilkley in Yorkshire:

Jim: "Dave senior, keen dart player, and son Doug – he's got the brains. Lovely to see you. And you've come all the way from Ilkley, that's super. But Doug's not your only son, is he, Dave?"

Dave: "No, Jim!"

Jim: "That's right. You've got another one called Gordon, haven't you?"

Dave: "That's right, Jim."

---

*There was a third incident. This was the only episode I can recall seeing in which someone won "Bully's Special Prize". But although I'm sure the winning couple were delighted to return to their flat in Bradford with a speedboat, it is also sadly irrelevant.

Jim: "So, tell us a little bit about Gordon. Tell us, what does he do?"

Dave: [proudly] "He's a welder, Jim."

Jim: [impressed] "That's good – he's working!"

A round of applause followed the release of this information, the object of which was clear – well done, Gordon. Unfortunately Doug and Dave are eliminated in the first round, leaving with just £70 and a "Bendy Bully", but that is not the last we see of them. The show's finale features a now-famous challenge: gamble the prizes you've won to win a fantastic mystery prize (typically a Mini Metro, Costa del Sol holiday or fitted kitchen). As Jim would put it every week: "Score 101 or more with six darts to win tonight's special prize, which is hiding behind Bully." Couple number one, having done well on Bully's prize board, decline the offer and leave with their video recorder, food mixer and something described as a "Tantalus". More amazingly, couple number two also decline to gamble, deeming £180 simply too much money to risk, and so return to Gateshead dreaming of what might have been. Their decision is greeted with a huge round of applause and Jim reassuring them that they've been "very wise". In 1983, £180 was obviously a lot of money, certainly too much to risk even on the once-in-a-lifetime opportunity to win a brand new car. Inflation does not tell the whole story, neither does the fact that people earned comparatively less in those days. It demonstrates an underlying conservatism and fear of the future that was common at this time. People were living in houses worth £10,000 and the idea that there may be another opportunity to get a free £180 to inject into the family budget was, frankly, ludicrous.

The modern enthusiasm for the business of making money and belief that you really can "make it" has created a more lackadaisical attitude to finance. Living in houses worth hundreds of thousands and with credit readily available, money has taken on a different (de)value. In 1983, entrepreneurship was still the preserve of a vague élite or at least of other people, not you. Today, anyone can set up a business, and there is a massive infrastructure armed with an extensive support network and huge pots of funding to ensure that as many people as possible do. Thatcher believed that the small businessperson was the key to the country's economic future. She once famously asked veteran *Guardian* columnist, the late Hugo Young, why on earth he didn't do something useful with his life, "like start a small business". Hugo didn't take the prime minister's advice but thousands did and, as a result, many of today's star performing companies – particularly those in the hi-tech and digital sectors – were spare-bedroom start-ups less than 20 years ago.

I don't know what percentage of these company workforces are staffed by City Slackers, but I do know that it's a lot. Frighteningly young boards of directors run many companies. There are more senior managers under the age of 40 on PLC boards than at any other time in history. As a consequence, opportunities for career progression in many of the disciplines that we have explored are limited, especially when you're often reporting to someone no more than a couple of years older than yourself. The contrast to this entrenchment is that today's employees are programmed to see standing still as moving backwards. If you're not moving up, you're moving out.

One CEO recently confessed to me that the biggest challenge facing his business was keeping staff motivated:

> Today, many people are only happy if they feel they're moving up the career ladder. Ultimately they'll come to a point beyond which they're not going to progress, and when that happens they start to feel unsettled. It's no longer enough to say, "You are good at your job, performing competently and we're happy with your performance." Do that and you'll find yourself being asked, "Yes, but where's my career going?" You either end up overpaying them so they can't go, or resigning yourself to the fact they'll be moving on.

He admits that his company is resigned to losing very good people because there's either no role for them to move into or, if there is, then it is one beyond their level of competence. Today's economic landscape and working practices do nothing to reward actual performance, loyalty, ability or success, but do much to reward the perception of experience, achievement and ability. A job-hopping CV, which will be seen invariably as a consolidated plan to garner experience and demonstrate career progression, can easily conceal incompetence, sloth and mediocrity. Seldom are these CVs taken as evidence of a poor spring-heeled performer keeping one step ahead of accountability or, more innocently, of someone who simply has reached the summit of their ability but is unable to accept this as fact. So, where do these people go? Obviously, into roles they are not suited to or capable of doing, and yet another City Slacker is created.

The months following the departure of a City Slacker can be a time of revelation and reflection. This post-mortem period is normally the first time that anyone considers: what exactly did Eric do while he was here? How surprisingly easy it is to cover for his absence and ultimately, what was it you were paying him all that money for? Unfortunately, resolution is less a question of dispensing with Eric's position altogether than making sure that you don't make the same mistakes when his replacement Ernie arrives. Although in truth, you probably will. By this time, Eric is moving on, his previous position no more than a footnote in a CV that will follow him to even bigger and better things. Like cream, it is inevitable that some City Slackers will rise to the top, some even going on to run companies.

In 1998 Emma Coyle was working for a UK video games publisher (let's call it ACE Games Limited) that, after a decade of growth and success, had got itself into financial trouble. Working at the company had been a great experience for many of the 400 or so staff, Emma included. For the most part, ACE Games had been a well-run business and a very pleasant place to work. The problems began when the company undertook a stock market flotation in the mid-1990s. The flotation did not go smoothly, ACE had not raised enough money to deliver its promises to the City, and this was compounded by poor sales performance which meant that, if it was to survive at all, it would have to find a buyer.

ACE was bought out by a large games company, Massive Inc. For the first ten years of its life, Massive had been pretty much a European equivalent to ACE, a well-run and well-regarded (if unspectacular) performer. Both companies had floated at around the same time, but whereas the London Stock Exchange had failed to get excited about ACE, its plans or its market, the BÖRSE simply couldn't get enough of Massive or its flamboyant CEO. Massive had built up a war chest of more than €500 million. ACE was just one of three companies that Massive bought out that month, along with a US publisher and a South East Asian development studio. Massive had gone from a small, provincial, 40-person, private enterprise, into a 4,000 employee-strong corporation in just over five years.

Acquisitions are never pleasant, and Emma spent the first few months trying to secure positions in the new organization for existing staff. When it came to discussion about her own future, she was mildly surprised and flattered to find that, rather than being emptied out, the CEO himself was quite keen to offer her a new position in the organization, he just wasn't sure what. With hindsight, Emma admits that she didn't cope with the change very well. Had she been willing to adopt a more pragmatic point of view, she concedes that she might have been able to carve out a decent position for herself. But she's glad that she didn't. Emma began to have misgivings just four days after the sale. Her team at ACE was set to attend the annual trade show in the US. Straight off the plane after a 13-hour flight they were bussed to a special presentation at a hotel, where they were given an in-depth analysis of the company strategy and a chance to meet their new colleagues. The culture at Massive was very different to that at ACE. During the meeting, all the attendees were invited to boo and hiss every time the name of its biggest competitor was mentioned. At the end, everybody was handed a list of dos and don'ts, which included the following sound advice:

1. Do remember you are representing the company!
2. Don't forget: "Massive is entertainment"!
3. Do remember to be in bed by 1am!
4. Don't forget to come to the Massive rooftop barbeque tomorrow night!

They were given name badges to wear at the show that read, rather tactlessly, "ex-ACE". Without the list, Emma might have forgotten to go to bed or to represent the company, but she will never forget the horror of the rooftop barbeque. It began with a series of sycophantic speeches made by directors that applauded the genius of the CEO, and was rounded off by the sight of the entire management team on stage "giving it large", like a herd of cows on ice to the company song; a high-energy ditty entitled "Massive Inc. Is Fun and Funky".

During the trade show Emma discovered three key facts about her new employer. First, the same management team that ran the original start-up company was running this multinational corporation, but with the addition of senior directors from the companies that they had purchased. Second, without exception, these purchased companies had been on their knees (or some would say, badly run) when Massive bought them with shareholder cash, and in every case they had paid way over the odds. Third, the quality of Massive's much-vaunted product line-up was much in keeping with the quality of its acquisitions and new executive appointments – it was complete crap. The board was full of fat cats congratulating themselves on their brilliant business acumen when they should have been thanking the Fates for their outrageous good fortune.

In the corporate scheme of things, running a small video games publisher in the 1990s was not an especially difficult or unique challenge. Certainly, running one successfully would have been beyond the abilities of most people, but only in the same way that running any moderately-sized company successfully would be beyond the ability of most people. Running a multinational corporation employing 4,000 people, however, is an entirely different proposition altogether. The new corporate Massive, it emerged, was going to be run along the same lines as a film studio, for no good reason other that the CEO appeared to like the idea of running a film studio, and certainly not because there were other companies successfully running the same model. The company operated three international studios: Massive Tinies, Massive Sports and Massive Adventure, each of which was responsible for developing different kinds of games. The finished product was then published by separate publishing or distribution operations in each territory.

Emma realized that knowledge of running a successful film business, let alone a successful games company, was clearly thin on the ground. To make up for lack of experience there were plenty of demonstrations of enthusiasm for the CEO's brilliant ideas. This blinded management to the fact that, because they had acquired a large number of companies in such a short space of time with no real experience of how to integrate them, there was now a huge amount of duplication. It was not difficult to find several people spread across several different departments in several different locations who were all trying to do the same job. The number of people apparently responsible for the same thing was staggering and, with no clear reporting lines, the politics within the organization were taking up more time than the process of developing, publishing and selling games.

For example, each studio allocated a marketing team to each title: usually a product manager and two product marketing executives, who were responsible for making sure that each title they delivered was "marketable". Their nebulous purpose was supposed to provide a conduit between the development team and each of the territory teams that would market the finished title. In practice they weren't responsible for developing the game – that was the role of the producer and their team – but they behaved as if they were. The fruit of their labours was delivered to a central marketing team at the company HQ, who in turn communicated it to the marketing teams in each of the territories. These territory teams could be pretty big. In the UK alone there was a marketing director, marketing manager, three product managers, six product marketing executives and no fewer than eight PR people.

The results of this strategy were wildly inefficient but surprisingly unchaotic, so things appeared to be going smoothly. This is because nobody was particularly keen to point out that they had nothing to do, or that there were several other people in the organization doing the same job. Inevitably, the best staff – those that could find other jobs – steadily began to drift away, leaving behind those who were either happy with the situation, or simply incapable of getting a job anywhere else, to run the show.

It is difficult to describe what eventually happened to Massive as anything other than an unmitigated disaster. When the numbers failed to add up, Massive gave up on the film studios idea and began shedding hundreds and hundreds of jobs in the process. The impact of its collapse was felt right across the industry. In the 1990s, the north of England had boasted its very own "Silicon Corridor" that employed thousands of people and supported a vibrant community of games developers. Today the sector has all but disappeared. In South Yorkshire alone between 2000 and 2003, over 600 jobs in the video games industry were lost.

The winners in this sorry tale were the senior executives, whose stock options and generous bonuses were, no doubt, ample compensation for the failure of their ludicrous business plan.

Yet, again, I make the point: Massive is not unique. Nor is it even a particularly ghastly offender. Unfortunately, Massive simply provides an example of what happens when City Slackers get the chance to run things with someone else's money. Invariably it may end in tears, but the tears are seldom theirs. The exit package will see to that.

The "exit" is a fundamental concept in modern business. Management consultants and business gurus will look at you aghast if you tell them that you haven't got one: "What do you mean, you haven't got an exit? You gotta have an exit! I mean, what's the point if you haven't got an exit?" The exit strategy: the point at which to get out, how you reach it and what you get. For companies (and for "companies", read "the people who run them") the exit usually involves a sale, a merger or even a stockmarket flotation. In practice, it generally means being able to get out the equity that you've built up, having done such a good job of running the business. Equally, it can mean being compensated for the equity that you would have built up, had you not proved to be incapable of running a bath, let alone a company like this one.

Towards the end of the 2004 football season, I was at a dinner with an accountant who represents a number of professional footballers. Over a few glasses of wine, we started talking about the problem facing football clubs relegated from the Premiership. I naively suggested that footballers' pay should be performance-related and that players at relegated clubs should be contractually obliged to take a pay cut. How he laughed: what kind of fool was I? On the contrary, he explained, were any of his clients unfortunate enough to find themselves playing for relegated clubs, their salary would actually increase as the club would compensate *them* for their lack of Premiership football. If nothing else, this story should give you something to consider next time you find yourself watching your brave lads, struggling for a draw that will see them avoid the drop. "Just one more mighty effort, lads! Keep this one out and we can all look forward to missing out on a pay rise."

But this situation is not very different to that in the corporate world. Recruiting for senior positions is an expensive and time-consuming exercise. The level of expertise required (and remember, this is an economy where experience, not ability, counts for everything) means that generally there are very few candidates capable of doing the job. They might not see an advertisement and even if they do, they may not be persuaded by it, so a headhunter is called in to find someone.

One of my clients, a publishing company, recently created a new position for a head of marketing. The MD estimated that there were possibly ten people in the UK with the right combination of experience to do the job, so rather than advertise, he appointed a headhunter not only to go and find the right person, but also to find out how much it was going to cost to get them. It's the kind of thing that happens with executive positions every day. For the City Slacker in this situation, it's time to celebrate. There will be many elements of the package to be discussed: options, pension, basic pay, holidays, company car and bonus, but none will be more important than the exit package – the insurance policy against relegation. All the good cards are held by the candidate. If the company is convinced that they are the right person for the job, it will want to convince them to move and will be scared that they won't. Besides, it's a beautiful day outside, and this is certainly no place to be discussing what happens when things go wrong – you've got every confidence that they'll be a great success. The exit pay-off looks like virtual rather than real money at this point, and the longer the notice period, the bigger the deterrent to the competition to headhunt them. After all, they're good, they're with us for the long haul and after all, shouldn't we be doing our best to keep hold of them? Giving them a few more options is hardly going to affect cashflow; it's good for them to have some skin in the business. It'll motivate them, keep them hungry.

A list citing examples where this strategy has backfired would fill this book several times over. When things do go wrong, getting rid of yesterday's golden boy is usually an onerous financial exercise in which the company ends up literally paying for nothing.

The UK's CEOs are the highest paid in the world after their American counterparts. During the past decade they have seen their salaries increase by an average of 288%. The UK's accountants do even better than the top dogs; they earn more money than their counterparts anywhere else in the world. So getting rid of these people when they fail to perform isn't going to be cheap. For running GlaxoSmithKline Beecham, Jan Leschly was paid £93 million in 2000. I'm sure his current performance means he's well worth his £46,700 an hour, but as he is probably on more than a month's notice, should the magic stop and he finds he's hit a bad patch, getting rid of him will prove a bit pricey*.

---

*Pricier even than the former CEO of EMI, Jim Fifield, who received a £12.4 million pay-off despite disastrous performance, presumably to soften the blow while he looked for a new position. It's a pity for him that he was based in the UK, where redundancy rates are around the lowest in the developed world at around 23% of fixed salary. He might have got even more if he'd been based abroad. Perhaps it's just evidence of his bad business acumen.

These implications were not lost on GlaxoSmithKline Beecham's shareholders who, less than 12 months later, inflicted an unprecedented defeat on the board. Over half of votes cast at the AGM were against approving the group's remuneration report, including the clauses about million-pound pay deals for its executives. Although shareholders had voted earlier by a clear majority to re-elect the GlaxoSmithKline Beecham board, the rejection of the executive pay plan was the biggest shareholder revolt of its kind in UK corporate history. The main bone of contention was a proposed "golden parachute" package for CEO Jean-Pierre Garnier. This is the payment that Garnier would receive if he lost his job: in other words, his insurance policy against failure. The Pensions Investment and Research Consultancy estimated this figure to be around $35.7 million (£22 million), which makes you wonder how much he would get if he performed well. The remuneration report also proposed putting all senior executives into rolling two-year contracts rather than the standard 12 months, effectively doubling the cost of getting rid of them overnight.

To me the message is clear: the people running GlaxoSmithKline (now GlaxoWellcome) are very aware of the difficulties facing modern businesses and, at the same time, have insight into their own ability to make a difference. They realize that, in the long term, they're screwed. They might ride their luck for a few years but come the inevitable downturn due to circumstances beyond their (or anyone else's) control, they'll be out of a job. So, while they are in control, they make sure that they plan appropriately for their exit. Karl Marx may have fallen out of fashion somewhat in recent times, but were he alive today, I'm sure he'd look at companies like GlaxoWellcome and Microsoft and say: "See, I told you so!"

GlaxoWellcome is by no means an isolated example of corporate greed. In 2003, the Trades Union Congress (TUC) highlighted the pay policy at HSBC. Under the company's remuneration rules, at least one of the bank's board directors could have made £20 million if he was dismissed. HSBC dismissed the criticism, issuing a statement arguing that the pay package for director William Aldinger represented good value for money. The TUC also identified 17 other British companies that were rewarding failure with vast golden parachute payments. The guilty parties included two other banks, Schroders and Barclays, City darlings Tesco, and a huge engineering conglomerate, Tomkins. I don't wish to sound like Tony Benn, but it's insane and obscene to think that any one person can be worth £20 million a year to a company. What's going to happen if William Aldinger gets knocked down as he's running for a bus?* Are we expected to believe that HSBC will simply crumble and die overnight? I wonder how much good value he'll appear to be in a few years time, should the company be struggling a little and need to bounce a few directors to appease its shareholders? Aldinger, who joined the bank's board after they bought a

---

*Perhaps an unlikely scenario given his earnings, but suspend your disbelief for a moment.

US lending company that he ran, will make millions in the event of his contract being terminated*.

In addition, it is going to get even more expensive to empty out top-level chaff. In 2003, executive pay in the top 100 UK companies went up by nearly 17%. The group that supplies these figures, the financial consultancy Incomes Data Services, maintains that a rapidly widening pay gap between executives and employees will cause inevitable internal tension, resulting in a loss of productivity. The pay of leading executives is no longer based on reality. It is driven by the pursuit of experience over ability and the misguided belief that if you pay someone £5 million a year, they must be worth £5 million a year.

In fact, like everybody else, the CEOs are simply making it up as they go along. CEOs don't have crystal balls (actually, some of them do) but they can't see into the future. Take any three annual reports from a public limited company and the chairperson's statement will say exactly the same things: that the company is concentrating on building upon its strengths and relationships in key markets; that it is focusing on eliminating weaknesses and obstacles; and finally that, in doing so, it hopes to get bigger. Former

---

*You'll like this. Since writing this chapter, Aldinger's contract with HSBC has been terminated. On 1 March 2005 HSBC announced profits of £9.6 billion, but it wasn't enough for the City. The analysts described the performance as lacklustre and the shareprice fell by 25p. The same day, the bank announced William Aldinger's departure. His take-home pay for less than three years in the job was $61 million.

Source: *Guardian*, 01.03.05 ("HSBC makes £9.6bn – but the City wanted more").

Labour cabinet minister and founder of the Social Democratic Party, the late Roy Jenkins, proposed a useful system for testing politicians' speeches. Jenkins suggested that you would know a speech is meaningless when saying the opposite would be ridiculous. It is a splendid test and it works equally well for company statements, announcements and annual reports: "The company is concentrating on eliminating its strengths and relationships in key markets. It is focusing on building on its weaknesses and obstacles and in doing so it hopes to get smaller."

Few companies are run by the book, least of all a business book. There will be lip service paid to the latest buzzwords, theories (almost all of which will be wrong) and clichés of management-speak, but outside the classrooms of Cranfield or Harvard, not many people are engaged in discussion about whether the company should operate a differentiation-focused or cost-leadership strategy*. If you read a business book from the 1970s you'll be surprised at how laughably and refreshingly simple it is. Certainly it will have little in common with the Stalinist case studies freely available from most corporate websites, which tell you everything the company feels you need to think about their latest successful product launch. It is much more difficult to find case studies for one of the more numerous products that have failed. It may be true that you can learn more from failure than you can from success, but today's business culture is geared exclusively towards learning only from success. Failures are to be

---

*Those that are almost certainly will be management consultants.

brushed away and forgotten; they are never talked about in polite conversation.

One thing that companies are very good at talking about is staff incentives. Many will pay management consultants top dollar to tell them – in no fewer than 10,000 words – that an incentivized, well-motivated workforce will be more productive. The story is somewhat different at the top. It is like an episode of the quiz show *Who Wants To Be A Millionaire?* where all the losers leave with £1 million; everyone wins and so no one bothers answering the questions. In many cases, there is no incentive to put the effort in and run the company well, but there is plenty to compensate you if you ever feel like telling them what they can do with your job.

I went to lunch recently with an old friend of mine, who is the marketing director at a FTSE 100 company. I hadn't seen him for a long time, and he was in high spirits during the meal. "I think I'm going to be made redundant," he told me excitedly. A new MD had arrived with new plans and his face just didn't fit. Happily, he'd worked out that he was going to clear almost £250,000 in redundancy and loyalty bonuses which, along with the proceeds from the sale of his house in Holland Park, would give him more than enough to "downsize". Or, specifically in his case, move back up north and work with his dad.

Brendan Barber, General Secretary of the TUC, summed up many people's frustration: "There are lots of people of talent who would relish the challenge of leading and running major companies in our country." He's right, of course – it's just that there are even more City Slackers relishing the challenge of securing a major pay-off.

10 | **City Slackers**

I have attempted to cover the phenomenon of City Slackers in an objective manner. Whether you view City Slackers as a good or a bad thing depends largely upon your own individual circumstances. I don't believe that it is useful or accurate to stereotype the entire population of City Slackers as a bunch of work-averse shysters who should be summarily dismissed. Of course, I have met many City Slackers for whom a hard day's work constituted only of having four pints at lunchtime. But by the same token, I have also known some supremely talented and capable individuals who were putting a great deal of time and effort into their own personal marketing campaigns and doing so with aplomb, creativity and effectiveness. Ask them how they are moving the company forwards and they'll laugh like a drain. Many in this group operate as City Slackers because there is no real work for them to do and they don't want to be made redundant.

No, the problem isn't with the slackers themselves, they are merely a symptom – or if you prefer, a bunch of entrepreneurs exploiting an opportunity. The problem is with the way that the corporate world operates: the way it measures performance, the way it manages people, the way it looks for experience over ability and the way it accepts and rewards failure, but most importantly, the way it tries to fill the world full of useless things.

Performance can be measured by many indicators. Being effective and getting things done is just one.*

Iain Duncan-Smith

It's not often that I – or anyone else for that matter – turns to the former Conservative Party leader Iain Duncan-Smith for pearls of wisdom, but this is possibly the most insightful thing that the self-confessed "quiet man" has ever said. I'm not entirely sure that he meant to be insightful and, as I actually read the quote in *Private Eye*, I'm prepared to take everything away from him and concede that it may have been something of a gaffe – "from the mouths of fools", one might say.

Large companies usually appraise their staff on an annual basis. These sessions involve the line manager assessing a member of staff's effectiveness against a long set of criteria. Have they shouldered additional responsibility? How customer-focused are they? Do they support the business's commitment to quality? In the vast majority of cases, these criteria are nonsense. Most employees have their performance tested against just two measures: are they a good bloke? And have they made the appraiser's life easier over the past 12 months?

There is cross-party political support for the free market economic system. That market forces are an intrinsically good thing is now taken as read. In that sense, should we really be surprised that a system which, by its very nature, encourages individualism and selfishness has led after just

---

*Source: *Waltham Forest Guardian*, 04.01.05 ("MP claims he is doing his best").

25 years to a generation of company people who actually couldn't give a toss about their company? Loyalty to inanimate objects – companies, organizations, ideologies or ideas – is anathema to secular society. Success is no longer the antithesis of failure. Failure is seen merely as an inevitable step on the way to success. Have enough failures and ultimately you will be successful. Launched a dot.com business and it failed? Then launch another one. Perhaps you'll have learned from your mistakes – at the very least you'll be able to sell your experience for a premium.

I used to live in a terraced house about two miles from the city centre. It was a great place to live but there was one minor downside. There was very little in the way of nightlife, just a couple of so-so pubs and an Indian restaurant at the bottom of the road. Unfortunately this restaurant closed down a few months after I moved in. Luckily, a new Indian restaurant opened in the same location a few months later. But then that closed down as well. It was replaced this time, not by an Indian, but by an Italian restaurant called Angelino's. This closed within six months, only to be replaced by an Egyptian restaurant. Then it became a Lebanese (not unlike Egyptian food, as I discovered), followed by a Spanish tapas bar, then a mysterious Aryan restaurant* before becoming an Italian again. I drove past the other day to see that La Trattoria Romantica had closed too but that the premises had already been sold subject to

---

*I wish I could tell you more about the Aryan Restaurant but I never went inside. It may amuse you to know that it was known colloquially as "Nietzsche's Philosophical Bar and Grill".

contract. What, I wondered, was the mindset of the previous seven owners? Clearly, they all felt that this was a great place for a restaurant, although if they'd simply crossed the road and knocked on my door, I could have explained exactly why it wasn't. What did they think made their restaurant idea so special, that it would succeed where so many others had failed? Perhaps it was just blind hubris in the face of all the evidence, or the well-meaning support of friends and family who had thought encouragingly that they would be "brilliant at running a restaurant".

Most things don't go well: 80% of businesses fail in the first year and 80% of the survivors will have failed within four years. Market consolidation means that many of those still-trading companies will either merge or be acquired. The economic landscape may be one approaching full employment, but that is where the similarities with the full employment of the 1960s ends. The climate is one of volatility; there is no such thing as a job for life and remaining with one company for too long will do nothing to help your marketability when the axe finally falls. And fall it will. Successful careers are built by drawing from a pool of broad expertise rather than from deep understanding of one particular function.

The flat corporate structures of modern organizations create the perfect environment for City Slackers to flourish. At the top is a cabal whose purpose, at least, is to drive the business forward strategically*. At the bottom of

---

*Although in practice, more often than not, it does this tactically and not strategically.

the pile are the producers: the people who actually do or make things. In the middle, with less well-defined purpose, is the aptly named middle management team with equally ill-defined responsibility. Collectively, these middle managers will be liable for things like quality, efficient production, sales or marketing but individually, it is highly unlikely that all of them will be functioning as a single team. At best, they will be dedicating much of their working day to ensuring that their own piece of the company machine is not implicated in the next market failure, and to maximizing its potential to deliver their own personal objectives: hopefully a promotion, but at the very least, the sense that they are performing a valuable and vital service for the business. Whatever, they will be thinking about themselves and only themselves. The less savvy will complain about long hours, poor pay or the difficulties that they experience with the new operating system on their company BlackBerry. Invariably they will want more money for doing the same job, and usually would appreciate a bit more authority, but certainly will not want to take on any extra responsibility.

If the emergence of the City Slacker is a symptom of anything, it is of the triumph of the individual over the collective. There is no such thing as a "company person" any more. Companies rewarding loyalty through the pay packets of key employees is nothing new, but loyalty is no longer a concept well understood in the workplace. A friend of mine, Robert Miller, once surprisingly tendered his resignation, having been offered twice his salary to go and work for one of our leading competitors. His CEO took this move quite badly – a personal betrayal by someone he'd previously considered honest and trustworthy. He felt that he had been shown a remarkable amount of disloyalty and that replacing one so capable was going to be very difficult. The fact that, from Robert's perspective, the company appeared to have been rewarding this loyalty and performance by paying him just 50% of his market value for the past three years was lost on the chief executive.

Things will not change until a failure is treated as a failure. The language of business has to change. Problems are simply that: problems. And they need solutions. They are not challenges or hurdles; the problem with some problems is they have no solution. Call them "challenges" if you like, it won't make them easier to solve. Experience is never a substitute for ability. It is true that you can learn more from failure than from success, but this is not to say that many people do. When asked for the secret of his success, Henry Ford famously replied: "Simple. Get up early, work late, win the lottery."

In January 2005, Ken Bates, erstwhile chairman of Chelsea FC, was being celebrated as the saviour of Leeds United: a club with vast debts and a debilitated playing staff that was struggling to avoid calling in the administrators. Thousands of column inches were dedicated to Bates and his millions, which, along with his vast experience, was seen as a recipe for returning Leeds to its former (almost) glories. I'm not sure what time Ken Bates goes to bed, or when he gets up, but what he certainly did do was win the lottery. Back in 2003, Chelsea

FC was also a club with vast debts (estimated to have been even bigger than those at Leeds) that was struggling to avoid calling in the administrators, when from out of nowhere Roman Abramovich arrived with a blank chequebook, a bottomless bank account and a desire to own a Premiership football club. He'd have preferred Spurs, but Chelsea was in more of a selling mood. Now Ken Bates finds himself regarded as possessing the kind of business acumen that only comes when you have millions of pounds in your pocket. Without any sign of a smile, Ken unveiled his plans for Leeds:

> It's going to be a tough job and the first task is to stabilize the cash flow and sort out the remaining creditors, but there is light at the end of a very long tunnel. For the past year it has been a matter of firefighting – now we can start running the club again.

At first this seems like a victory for common sense: balance the books and we've a sure-fire recipe for success, what could be simpler? Just one question Ken: what with? Wherever the necessary cash is going to flow from, it certainly won't be from the gate receipts, Sky TV or the Champions League. Moreover, this "prudence first" strategy is not something that Ken made himself famous for at his previous club. Maybe he's planning to build a "Leeds Village". Now, where did I put that Russian oligarch's number …?

It's safe to say that, for the time being at least, City Slackers will continue to thrive and prosper. There is everything to encourage them and nothing to stop them.

City Slackers are not just running departments – they're running companies, often quite major ones. Fear of failure is as irrational as fear of the bogeyman. Your choice is simply whether you swim with or against them. Maybe you're a slacker already and just don't realize it.

Being a City Slacker is more about what motivates you to take decisions than anything else. The City Slacker and the company may enjoy a transient symbiotic relationship, but in time their objectives will diverge. The more City Slackers an organization employs, the more inefficient it will become. Great performance needs to rely on more than happenstance, but in many organizations, success is down to just that. Good fortune is never acknowledged as a major contributing factor to performance; it is wrapped in hindsight that gives it an unworthy strategic weight: a great product comes along at the right time, a chance meeting results in a new blue-chip client, an employee has a visionary "blue sky" idea: these things happen all the time but can never be planned, whatever the business books tell you.

One running joke in the popular TV series *Friends* concerned the occupation of the character Chandler. Nobody knew what Chandler did for a living, and he himself found it impossible to explain. The situation is funny (unlike this analysis) because it is something to which most of us can relate. In this age of new specialists, many of us know at least somebody who has one of these jobs. But if you don't know categorically the *outcomes* that everyone in your organization is responsible for, you can take it as read that the work they are doing won't impact positively on your organization's performance.

191

In the end, the mind of the City Slacker begins to work differently. They stop thinking about the company altogether and concern themselves only with the way that they are perceived. Nick Barnes runs his own business as a corporate headhunter. He spends his life shuffling a pack of very senior executives and dealing them out to clients who have £100K vacancies that need filling. He takes 20% for his trouble. A few years ago he was asked to find a senior marketing executive for a multinational music television company. His candidate, Jason Barber, had been the marketing director of a film and video distributor for three years and was now looking to take the step across into the music business. Jason's performance at the interview was obviously paramount, not only in terms of securing the job for himself but also for Nick's not insubstantial commission. On the day of the interview, Nick came out of a meeting to find no fewer than six messages from Jason on his mobile phone. Each message was slightly more anxious than the last, and each one requested that Nick ring Jason urgently. Understanding that Jason probably needed a bit of last-minute advice, Nick returned his call immediately to see how he could help.

"Thank God you rang," gasped Jason, "I really need your advice. You know these people better than me, what should it be this afternoon: the Paul Smith or the Armani?"

Jason got the job. I think he went with the Paul Smith.